DEBBIE MUMM'S.

COLORS from NATURE

DEBBIE MUMM

Dear Friends,

Nature gives us endless beauty to enjoy and to use as inspiration – and that is what this book is about. We looked at some of the beautiful colors and combinations of colors that nature gives us and used these as inspiration to create quilt, craft and decorating projects. The journey was just as enjoyable as the results.

From the desert to the seashore, from the forest floor to a sun-filled meadow, we have explored many types of terrain for this book without ever leaving the studio. Selecting the photos was a fun process. However, interpreting these images into quilt designs was what really gave us a buzz of excitement. We were challenged and ultimately pleased to capture the essence of the landscape using color, fabric and simple block designs.

Please take a few moments to look through this book to enjoy the scenic views and inspiring photography and projects, all from the comfort of your easy chair. I think you'll look at everything a little differently after you do – and perhaps, with even more clarity, be able to recognize the creative inspiration that nature has to offer. I hope these projects, as well, continue to be a resource of ideas for you over the years. Enjoy!

With Appreciation,

Debbie Mumm

TABLE
of Contents

Velvety hues evoke verdant grasses and a lazy river in this harmonic grouping of projects. Olive green, brown, moss, and blue, blur the boundaries between water and land in this enticing grouping.

RIVER
Reflections

Reflections Wall Quilt Finished Size: 43½" x 43½"	FIRST CUT		SECOND CUT	
	Number of Strips or Pieces	Dimensions	Number of Pieces	Dimensions
Fabric A Appliqué Background ⅓ yard each of 2 fabrics	1*	10" x 42" *Cut for each fabric	2*	10" x 12½"
Fabric B Water ⅛ yard each of 2 fabrics	1*	3" x 42" *Cut for each fabric	2*	3" x 12½"
Fabric C Accent Border ¼ yard	5	1" x 42"	2 3 2	1" x 26" 1" x 25" 1" x 12½"
Fabric D Block 1 & 2 Dark Accents ¼ yard	2	3½" x 42"	12 10	3½" squares 2¾" squares
Fabric E Block 1 & 2 Light Accents ⅓ yard	1 1	6½" x 42" 2" x 42"	6 10	6½" squares 2" squares
Fabric F Block 1 & 2 Background ¾ yard	3 2 3	3½" x 42" 2¾" x 42" 2" x 42"	6 12 10 10 20	3½" x 6½" 3½" squares 2¾" x 5" 2¾" squares 2" x 5"
Fabric G Block 2 Triangle ⅓ yard	2	5" x 42"	10	5" squares
Fabric H Border Side & Corner Triangles ⅓ yard	1	9¾" x 42"	3** 2***	9¾" squares **Cut twice diagonally for Side Triangles 5⅛" squares ***Cut once diagonally for Corner Triangles
Fabric I Border Side & Corner Triangles ½ yard	1 1	9¾" x 42" 5⅛" x 42"	3** 6***	9¾" squares **Cut twice diagonally for Side Triangles 5⅛" squares ***Cut once diagonally for Corner Triangles
Binding ½ yard	5	2¾" x 42"		

Backing - 2¾ yards
Batting - 49" x 49"
Black Beads (for eyes) - 4

Duck, Cattail & Leaf Appliqués - Assorted scraps
Lightweight Fusible Web - 1½ yards

Fabric Requirements and Cutting Instructions

Read all instructions before beginning and use ¼"-wide seam allowances throughout. Read Cutting Strips and Pieces on page 92 prior to cutting fabric.

Getting Started

The gentle current of a river invites migrating ducks to our landscape scene. This wall quilt features center blocks with appliquéd ducks and incorporates two smaller pieced blocks in this unique border treatment. Duck blocks measure 12½" square (unfinished). Each border block measures 6½" (unfinished). Refer to Accurate Seam Allowance on page 92. Whenever possible use the Assembly Line Method on page 92. Press seams in direction of arrows.

Making the Center Unit

1. Sew one 10" x 12½" Fabric A piece to one 3" x 12½" Fabric B piece as shown. Press. Make four, two of each combination.

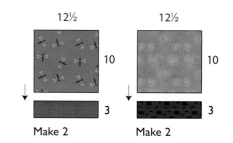

Make 2   Make 2

. Sew one 1" x 12½" Fabric C strip between two units from step 1, one of each combination. Press. Make two, one of each combination. Sew these units and three 1" x 25" Fabric C strips together as shown. Press.

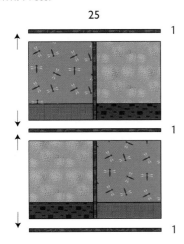

3. Referring to layout, sew two 1" x 26" Fabric C strips to sides of unit from step 2. Press.

Adding the Appliqués

Refer to appliqué instructions on page 93. Our instructions are for Quick-Fuse Appliqué but if you prefer hand appliqué, add ¼"-wide seam allowance.

1. Use patterns on pages 9-11 to trace ducks, cattails, and leaves on paper side of fusible web. Use appropriate fabrics to prepare all appliqués for fusing.

2. Refer to photo on page 5 and layout to position and fuse appliqués to quilt. Finish appliqué edges with machine satin stitch or other decorative stitching as desired.

Making the Pieced Border

1. Sew together one 3½" Fabric D square to one 3½" Fabric F square. Press. Sew one 3½" x 6½" Fabric F piece to this unit as shown. Press. Make six.

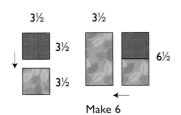

Make 6

Reflections
Wall Quilt
Finished Size: 43½" x 43½"

Handsomely-hued ducks are reflected in the water on this intriguing wall quilt. Border blocks mimic both fish and fowl and create a frame for the center scene. The masculine color scheme and outdoors theme make this project a great guy gift.

2. Refer to Quick Corner Triangles on page 92. Making a quick corner triangle unit, sew one 6½" Fabric E square to unit from step 1, noting orientation of unit. Press.

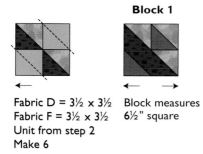

Fabric E = 6½ x 6½
Unit from step 1
Make 6

3. Making quick corner triangle units, sew one 3½" Fabric D square and one 3½" Fabric F square to unit from step 2 as shown. Press. Make six and label Block 1. Block measures 6½" square.

Block 1

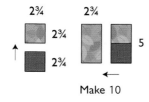

Fabric D = 3½ x 3½   Block measures
Fabric F = 3½ x 3½   6½" square
Unit from step 2
Make 6

4. Sew together one 2¾" Fabric F square and one 2¾" Fabric D square. Press. Sew one 2¾" x 5" Fabric F piece to this unit as shown. Press. Make ten.

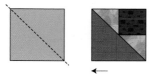

Make 10

5. Making a quick corner triangle unit, sew one 5" Fabric G square to unit from step 4 as shown, noting orientation of unit. Press. Make ten.

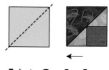

Fabric G = 5 x 5
Unit from step 4
Make 10

6. Sew one 2" x 5" Fabric F piece to one unit from step 5 as shown. Press. Make ten.

Make 10

7. Sew one 2" Fabric E square to one 2" x 5" Fabric F piece as shown. Press. Sew this unit to one unit from step 6 as shown. Press. Make ten and label Block 2. Block measures 6½" square.

Make 10

Block 2

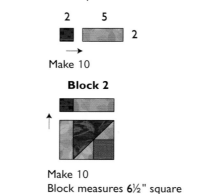

Make 10
Block measures 6½" square

8. **Note:** For steps 8-15 press seams towards triangles. Sew one Fabric I corner triangle to one Block 1. Press. Sew this unit between one Fabric I side triangle and one Fabric H corner triangle as shown. Press. Make two and label Unit 1.

Unit 1

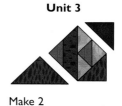

Make 2

9. Sew one Block 1 between one Fabric H and one Fabric I side triangles as shown. Press. Make two and label Unit 2.

Unit 2

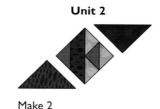

Make 2

10. Sew one Block 1 to one Fabric H corner triangle. Press. Sew this unit between one Fabric H side triangle and one Fabric I corner triangle as shown. Press. Make two and label Unit 3.

Unit 3

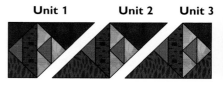

Make 2

11. Arrange and sew together one unit each from steps 8-10 as shown to make a row. Press. Make two. Referring to photo on page 5 and layout on page 7, arrange and sew to top and bottom of quilt making sure Fabric H is toward center of quilt. Press seams open.

Unit 1   Unit 2   Unit 3

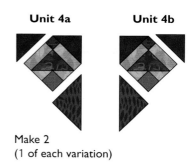

Make 2

12. Sew one Block 2 to one Fabric I corner triangle. Press. Sew this unit between one Fabric I corner triangle and one Fabric H side triangle. Press. Make two, one of each variation as shown. Label Unit 4a and 4b.

Unit 4a   **Unit 4b**

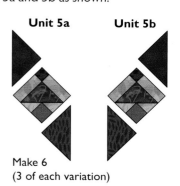

Make 2
(1 of each variation)

13. Sew one Block 2 between one Fabric H and one Fabric I side triangle. Press. Make six, three of each variation. Label Unit 5a and 5b as shown.

Unit 5a   **Unit 5b**

Make 6
(3 of each variation)

4. Sew one Block 2 to one Fabric I corner triangle. Press. Sew this unit between one Fabric I side setting triangle and one Fabric I corner triangle as shown. Press. Make two, one of each variation as shown. Label Unit 6a and 6b.

Unit 6a   **Unit 6b**

Make 2
(1 of each variation)

5. Arrange and sew together one Unit 4a, three of Unit 5a and one Unit 6a as shown. Press. Repeat using Units 4b, 5b, and 6b. Referring to photo on page 5 and layout on page 7, sew rows to sides of quilt. Press.

Layering and Finishing

1. Cut backing crosswise into two equal pieces. Sew pieces together lengthwise to make one 49" x 80" (approximate) backing piece. Press and trim to 49" x 49".

2. Referring to Layering the Quilt on page 94, arrange and baste backing, batting, and top together. Hand or machine quilt as desired.

3. Referring to Binding the Quilt on page 94, sew 2¾" x 42" binding strips end-to-end to make one continuous 2¾"-wide binding strip. Bind quilt to finish.

4. Referring to photo on page 5, sew beads for eyes on quilt. Add other embellishments as desired.

River Runner (Page 12)
Enlarge Cattail patterns by 110%
Permission is granted by Debbie Mumm Inc.
to copy page 9 to successsfully complete this project.

Make 2 and 2 Reversed

**Reflections
Wall Quilt**

**Cattail
Make 3 and 3 Reversed**

**Leaf Sets
Make 2 and 2 Reversed**

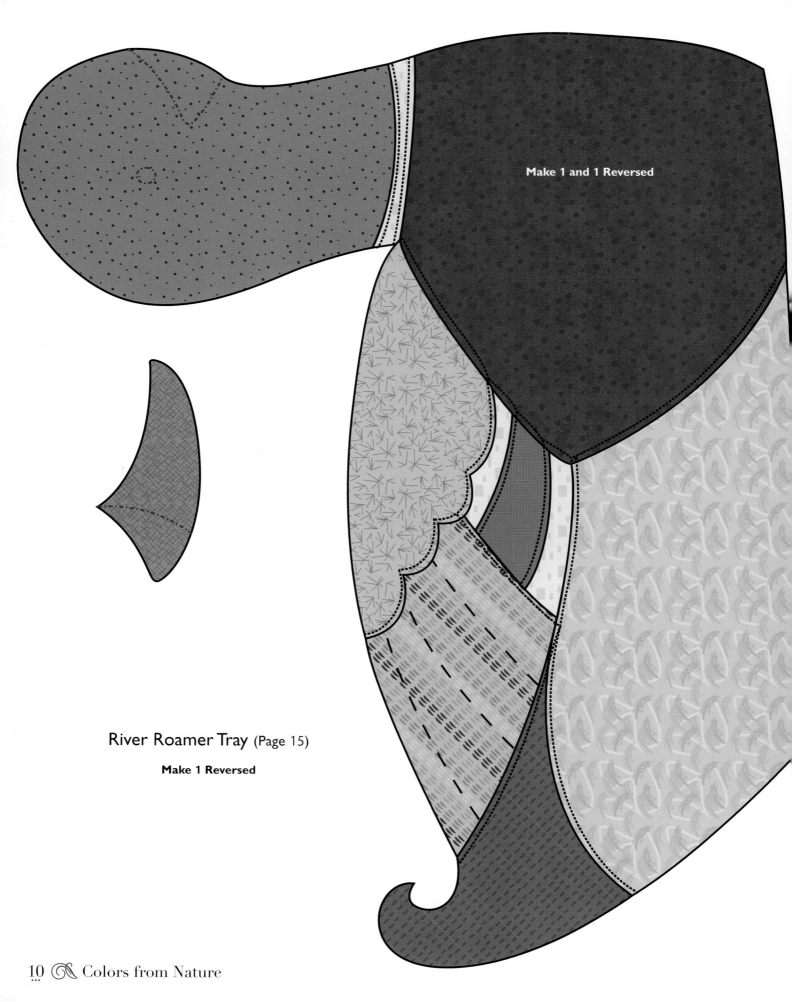

Make 1 and 1 Reversed

River Roamer Tray (Page 15)

Make 1 Reversed

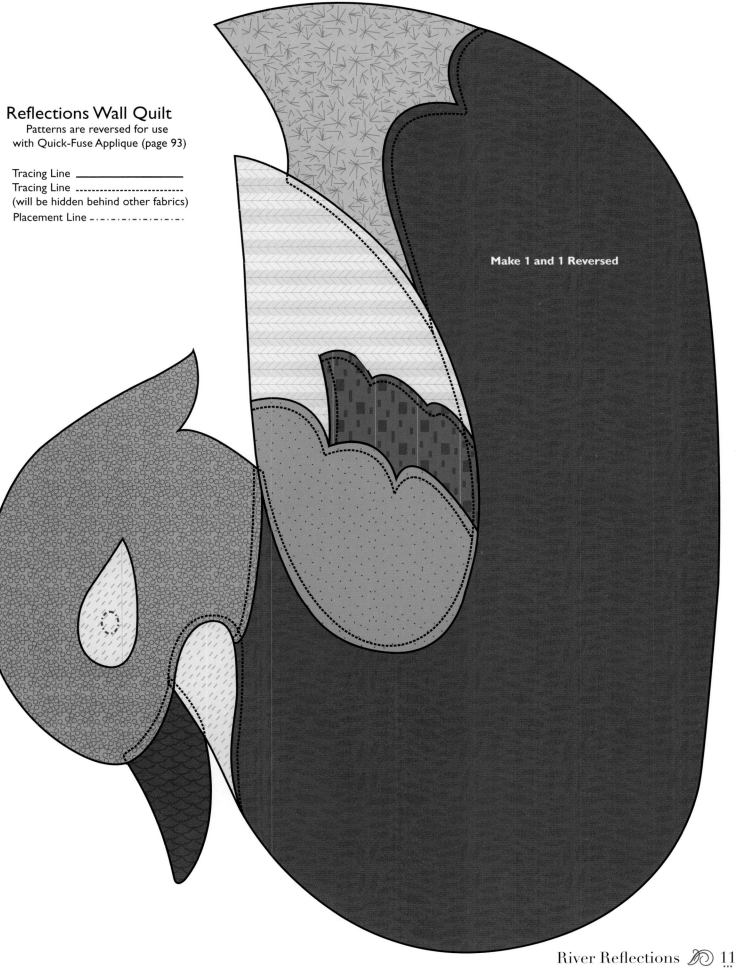

Reflections Wall Quilt
Patterns are reversed for use
with Quick-Fuse Applique (page 93)

Tracing Line ————————
Tracing Line ------------------------
(will be hidden behind other fabrics)
Placement Line —·—·—·—·—·—

Make 1 and 1 Reversed

RIVER
Runner

Getting Started

Bring memories of times spent gathering cattails by the river's edge to your table by making this easy-to-construct wool table runner. Read all instructions before beginning.

Cutting the Background Fabric

1. Using a compass point and yardstick with points set 7¼" apart, draw a half circle on paper.

2. Cut Background piece 14½" x 30". Using half circle pattern from step 1, cut each end to make an oval background piece.

Adding the Appliqués

Refer to appliqué instructions on page 93. Our instructions are for Quick-Fuse Appliqué, but if you prefer hand appliqué, add ¼"-wide seam allowance when using cotton fabrics.

1. Enlarge Cattail patterns on page 9 to 110%. Trace two regular and two reversed of each cattail element on paper side of fusible web. Use appropriate fabrics to prepare all appliqués for fusing.

2. Refer to photo on page 13 to position and fuse appliqués to background piece. **Note:** Our cattails were placed ¾" from background edge with stem and leaf ends butted together.

3. Using a straight stitch for wool fabric, stitch each leaf lengthwise down center. Finish cattail edges and stems with machine satin stitch or other decorative stitching as desired. If using cotton appliqués, finish all edges with satin or decorative stitches.

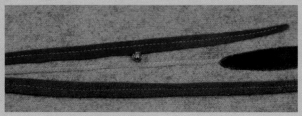

Layering and Finishing

1. Layer backing, yarn, and background pieces together, placing yarn between layers. Stitch through all layers using a machine blanket stitch along background outside edge or stitch as desired. We used a yarn with a wider width. If desired as an alternative, couch yarn (page 95) in place along background piece edge prior to layering.

2. Trim backing piece approximately ¼"-½" away from yarn edge.

3. Refer to photo on page 13 to arrange and sew assorted beads to quilt.

- Background—½ yard wool
- Leaf Appliqués—Assorted wool scraps
- Cattails & Stem Appliqués—Assorted wool scraps
- Backing—½ yard wool
- Lightweight Fusible Web—½ yard
- Yarn—2½ yards
- Assorted Beads
- Yardstick & Compass Points

SUPPLIES

RIVER
Centerpiece

SUPPLIES

- Glass Platter or Plate
- Assorted Seed and Bugle Beads in River Colors
- Sea Glass or Glossy Stones
- Clear Glass Marbles
- Glass Votive Holders
- Ivory Votives

Creating the Centerpiece

Place votives in votive holders and place as desired in glass platter.

Sprinkle seed and bugle beads in the bottom of the platter.

Add clear glass marbles and sea glass or glossy stones.

Enjoy!

Note: When done with centerpiece, separate items and save beads for jewelry projects or quilt embellishments.

Sometimes the simple things are those most treasured. Cattails sway in the breeze on this quick and easy wool table runner. The simplicity of the scene is reflected in the centerpiece where candles appear to float in a river of beads and sea glass.

FISH TALES
Memory Catcher

Catch the big ones...memories that is...in a special holder that's just right for show and tell. We used a tin CD holder to create an accordion fold memory catcher to display photos of fun riverside adventures.

Decorating the Tin

1. Paint cover and base of tin using no-prep metal paint.

2. Trim background papers to fit tin cover. Ink or tear edges. Glue to cover.

3. Adhere "Fish Tales" title sticker using foam mounting tape.

4. Use craft glue to adhere ribbons, metal embellishments, and fishing lure.

Creating the Accordion Insert

1. Trim cardstock pieces to fit inside tin. Round corners, if necessary.

2. Decorate pages using photos and a variety of embellishments and papers.

3. Lay ½ of the pages face down in a row, allowing approximately ¼" between pages. Lay length of ribbon across middle of pages extending ends approximately 10" from outside pages. Apply glue to top and bottom edges of wrong side of pages. Adhere remaining pages face up covering the ribbon and aligning edges with glued pages. Ribbon should slide freely through center of pages.

4. Fold up pages accordion-style and tie ribbon ends.

SUPPLIES

- **Tin Container with Lid**
- **No-Prep Metal Paint**
- **Ink Pad**
- **Cardstock**
- **Assorted Specialty Papers**
- **Assorted Ribbons**
- **Assorted Metal, Sticker, Fiber & Artificial Floral Embellishments**
- **Photos**
- **Craft Glue**
- **Foam Mounting Tape**
- **Fishing Lure**

RIVER
Roamer Tray

Remember fun summer days on the river every time you use this handsome tray. Perfect for serving cold beverages or carrying treats to the patio, this tray is just ducky!

Making the Tray

1. Using duck pattern (reversed) on page 10 and referring to Quick Fuse Applique and Applique Pressing Sheet on page 93, use fabric scraps to create duck appliqué.

2. Remove tray handles (if any). Sand tray lightly and remove residue with damp cloth. Paint tray with gesso and allow to dry.

3. Thin Wedgwood Blue paint with water and wash paint over bottom of tray. Allow to dry. Thin Blue Bayou paint with water and wash over entire bottom of tray and allow to dry. Use Scotch Magic Tape to tape off water area. Using thinned Blue Bayou paint, wash over water area alone to achieve a darker color. Allow to dry.

4. Paint each side of tray a different color. We used Burnt Umber, Spice Brown, Hauser Green Light, and Avocado. Allow paint to dry between each color. Several coats may be necessary for good coverage.

5. Paint outside sides of tray as desired and use Burnt Orange paint for top rim. Allow to dry.

6. Coat back side of duck appliqué with Mod Podge and carefully place and smooth duck onto bottom of tray. Cover entire bottom of tray with Mod Podge being careful when painting over duck. Allow to dry. Cover bottom of tray with a second coat of Mod Podge. Allow to dry thoroughly.

7. Apply Antiquing Medium to inside of tray and use a clean lint-free cloth to wipe off as desired. Allow to dry. Apply Antiquing Medium to outside of tray, wiping off or adding more as desired. Allow to dry. Apply several coats of exterior varnish, allowing tray to dry well between applications. Reattach handles.

SUPPLIES

- **Wooden Tray**
- **Assorted Fabric Scraps**
- **Delta Ceramcoat® Acrylic Craft Paints**
  Wedgwood Blue, Blue Bayou, Spice Brown and Burnt Umber
- **Americana® Acrylic Craft Paints**
  Avocado, Hauser Green Light, and Burnt Orange
- **Folkart® Antiquing Medium by Plaid®**
  Woodn' Bucket Brown
- **White Gesso**
- **Lightweight Fusible Web—⅓ yard**
- **Mod Podge® Satin**
- **Assorted Paint Brushes**
- **Delta Ceramcoat® Exterior Spray Varnish**
- **Scotch® Magic™ Tape**
- **Sandpaper**

Frolicking poppies and daisies sway in the breeze in this group of sun-drenched projects. Ivory, yellow, red, and green compose a summertime color scheme.

MEADOW
Melodies

Lap Quilt

Meadow Flowers Lap Quilt Finished Size: 57½" x 81½"	FIRST CUT		SECOND CUT	
	Number of Strips or Pieces	Dimensions	Number of Pieces	Dimensions
Fabric A Foilage Small Flower Backgrounds ⅜ yard each of 11 fabrics	3*	3½" x 42" *Cut for each fabric	24*	3½" squares
Fabric B Large Flower Block Background ½ yard each of 3 fabrics	2* 2*	4" x 42" 3½" x 42" *Cut for each fabric	12* 12*	4" squares 3½" squares
Fabric C Large Flower Block Accent Foilage ⅙ yard each of 3 fabrics	1*	4" x 42" *Cut for each fabric	6*	4" squares
Fabric D Large Flower Petals ¼ yard each of 3 fabrics	2*	3½" x 42" *Cut for each fabric	12*	3½" x 6½"
Fabric E Large Flower Small Petals ⅙ yard each of 3 fabrics	1*	4" x 42" *Cut for each fabric	6*	4" squares
Fabric F Large Flower Center Petals ¼ yard each of 3 fabrics	2*	3½" x 42" *Cut for each fabric	12*	3½" squares
Fabric G Block 4 and 5 Petals ¼ yard each of 2 fabrics	2*	3½" x 42" *Cut for each fabric	20*	3½" squares
Fabric H Block 6 and 7 Petals ¼ yard each of 2 fabrics	2*	3½" x 42" *Cut for each fabric	16*	3½" squares
First Border ⅓ yard	7	1¼" x 42"		
Second Border ¼ yard	7	1" x 42"		
Outside Border ⅞ yard	8	3½" x 42"		
Binding ⅔ yard	8	2¾" x 42"		
Backing - 4⅞ yards		Batting - 63" x 87"		

Fabric Requirements and Cutting Instructions

Read all instructions before beginning and use ¼"-wide seam allowances throughout. Read Cutting Strips and Pieces on page 92 prior to cutting fabric.

Getting Started

The scattering of flowers against a field of green foliage brings the dazzling meadow to your home in this lap quilt. Large and small floral blocks and a variety of green foliage blocks interplay to make a scrappy quilt. Each block measures 12½" square (unfinished). Refer to Accurate Seam Allowance on page 92. Whenever possible use the Assembly Line Method on page 92. Press seams in the direction of arrows.

Making the Large Flower Blocks

This block is made in three different shades: dark, medium, and light. Block 1 uses the darkest shades of each fabric.

1. Draw diagonal line on wrong side of one 4" Fabric C square. Place marked square and one 4" Fabric B square right sides together. Sew scant ¼" away from drawn line on **both** sides to make half-square triangles as shown. Make six. Cut **on** drawn line. Press. Square units to 3½". This will make twelve half-square triangle units.

Fabric C = 4 x 4   Square to 3½"
Fabric B = 4 x 4   Make 12
Make 6   Half-square triangles

Draw diagonal line on wrong side of one 4" Fabric E square. Place marked square and one 4" Fabric B square right sides together. Sew scant ¼" away from drawn line on **both** sides to make half-square triangles as shown. Make six. Cut **on** drawn line. Press. Square units to 3½". This will make twelve half-square triangle units.

Fabric E = 4 x 4   Square to 3½
Fabric B = 4 x 4   Make 12
Make 6   Half-square triangles

Refer to Quick Corner Triangles on page 92. Making quick corner triangle units, sew one 3½" Fabric B square and one 3½" Fabric F square to one 3½" x 6½" Fabric D piece as shown. Press. Make twelve.

Fabric B = 3½ x 3½
Fabric F = 3½ x 3½
Fabric D = 3½ x 6½
Make 12

Sew one unit from step 1 to one unit from step 2 as shown. Press. Make twelve. Sew one of these units to one unit from step 3 as shown. Press. Make twelve.

Make 12

Make 12

Sew two units from step 4 together as shown. Press. Make six. Sew these units together in pairs as shown. Refer to Twisting Seams on page 92. Press. Make three and label Block 1. Block measures 12½" square.

Block 1

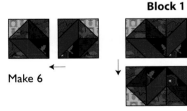

Make 6

Make 3
Block measures
12½" square

Meadow Flowers
Lap Quilt
Finished Size: 57½" x 81½"

Pieced blocks combine for a festival of color and design on this winsome lap quilt. Like a sun-drenched field of flowers, subtle variations of color and pattern create a wild floral wonderland.

6. Refer to steps 1-5 to make two medium blocks and label Block 2. Refer to steps 1-5 to make three light blocks and label Block 3.

Block 2   **Block 3**

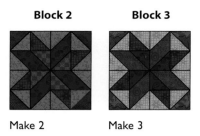

Make 2   Make 3

Making the Small Flower Blocks

Four different fabrics (G and H) are used for the small flowers and a variety of greens (A) for the foliage background.

1. Refer to Quick Corner Triangles on page 92. Making a quick corner triangle unit, sew one 3½" Fabric A square to one 3½" Fabric G square as shown. Press. Make twenty.

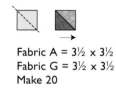

Fabric A = 3½ x 3½
Fabric G = 3½ x 3½
Make 20

2. Sew units from step 1 together in pairs as shown. Press. Make ten. Sew two of these units together as shown. Referring to Twisting Seams page 92, Press. Make five and label Unit 1.

Unit 1

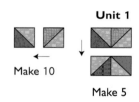

Make 10

Make 5

3. Repeat steps 1 and 2 to make five of Unit 2 (Fabrics A and G), four of Unit 3 (Fabrics A and H), and four of Unit 4 (Fabrics A and H).

Unit 2   **Unit 3**   **Unit 4**

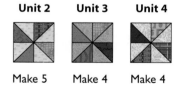

Make 5   Make 4   Make 4

4. Sew different 3½" Fabric A squares together in pairs as shown. Press. Make thirty-six. Sew these units together in pairs as shown. Press. Make eighteen.

3½   3½

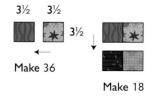

3½

Make 36

Make 18

5. Sew one Unit 1 to one unit from step 4 as shown. Press. Make five. Repeat using units from step 4 to make eighteen, five using Unit 2, four using Unit 3, and four using Unit 4. Label all Unit 5 and set four aside for Foilage Blocks.

Unit 5

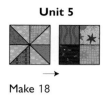

Make 18

6. Referring to photo on page 17 and layout on page 19, sew two units from step 5 together to make Small Flower Block. Refer to Twisting Seams on page 92. Press. Make seven and label Block 4. Block measures 12½" square.

Block 4

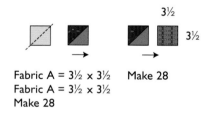

Make 7
(each using a different Small Flower Unit combination)
Block measures 12½" square

Making the Foliage Blocks

1. Refer to Quick Corner Triangles on page 92. Making a quick corner triangle unit, sew one 3½" Fabric A square to one different 3½" Fabric A square as shown. Press. Make twenty-eight. Sew one of these units to one 3½" Fabric A square as shown. Press. Make twenty-eight.

3½

3½

Fabric A = 3½ x 3½   Make 28
Fabric A = 3½ x 3½
Make 28

2. Sew two different 3½" Fabric A squares together as shown. Press. Make twenty-eight. Sew one of these units to one unit from step 1 as shown. Refer to Twisting Seams on page 92. Press. Make twenty-eight.

3½   3½

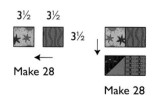

3½

Make 28

Make 28

Sew units from step 2 together in pairs as shown, checking orientation of units prior to sewing. Press. Make fourteen. Label Unit 6. Sew one Unit 6 to one Unit 5 as shown. Twist seams. Press. Make four. Label Block 5. Block measures 12½" square.

Unit 6

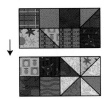

Make 14

Block 5

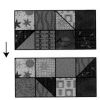

Make 4
Block measures 12½" square

4. Sew two of Unit 6 together as shown, checking orientation of units prior to sewing. Twist Seams. Press. Make five. Label Block 6. Block measures 12½" square.

Block 6

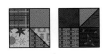

Make 5
Block measures 12½" square

Assembly

For assembly in each of the following steps refer to photo on page 17 and layout on page 19. Press odd rows to the left and even rows to the right.

1. Arrange and sew together two of Block 4, one Block 2, and one Block 6. Press and label Row 1.

2. Arrange and sew together one Block 1, one Block 4, one Block 3, and one Block 5. Press. Make two and label Rows 2 and 6.

3. Arrange and sew together one Block 5, two of Block 6, and one Block 4. Press and label Row 3.

4. Arrange and sew together one Block 4, one Block 3, one Block 6, and one Block 1. Press and label Row 4.

5. Arrange and sew together one Block 2, one Block 6, one Block 4, and one Block 5. Press and label Row 5.

6. Arrange and sew together Rows 1, 2, 3, 4, and 5. Press.

Adding the Borders

1. Sew 1¼" x 42" First Border strips together end-to-end to make one continuous 1¼"-wide First Border strip. Referring to Adding the Borders on page 94, measure quilt through center from side to side. Cut two 1¼"-wide First Border strips to this measurement. Sew to top and bottom of quilt. Press seams toward border.

2. Measure quilt through center from top to bottom including borders just added. Cut two 1¼"-wide First Border strips to this measurement. Sew to sides of quilt. Press.

3. Refer to steps 1 and 2 to join, measure, trim, and sew 1"-wide Second Border and 3½"-wide Outside Border strips to top, bottom, and sides of quilt. Press.

Layering and Finishing

1. Cut backing crosswise into two equal pieces. Sew pieces together lengthwise to make one 80" x 87" (approximate) backing piece. Press and trim to 63" x 87".

2. Referring to Layering the Quilt on page 94, arrange and baste backing, batting, and top together. Hand or machine quilt as desired.

3. Refer to Binding the Quilt on page 94. Sew 2¾" x 42" binding strips end-to-end to make one continuous 2¾"-wide binding strip. Bind quilt to finish.

MINI MEADOWS
Wall Art

Carry the melodies of the meadow throughout your home by creating these whimsical wall pieces. Beads, ribbon, and fabric combine to make these crafty and creative accents.

Making the Wall Art

1. Refer to General Painting instructions on page 95. Lightly sand wooden frames and remove residue using a damp cloth.

2. Apply a thin coat of gesso to each frame to prepare surface for painting. Allow to dry.

3. Decide on paint treatment for each frame. We chose to paint one Apple Green, another Golden Straw; and the third with stripes. Two or more coats of paint may be needed for good coverage. Always allow paint to dry thoroughly between coats.

Apple Green Frame

1. When Apple Green paint is dry, spray frame with matte varnish and allow to dry. Following manufacturer's directions, apply antiquing medium, wiping away excess or adding more to achieve color desired. When thoroughly dry, spray frame with final coat of matte varnish.

2. We chose to feature a square of a fun fabric in this frame. Cut a piece of cardboard to fit inside frame then cover with a square of fabric, wrapping ends to the back and securing with tape or a Lacing Stitch (page 95).

3. Using photo as inspiration, wrap ribbon around frame, securing in the back with Jewel Glue. Glue assorted beads to frame and fabric square as desired.

Golden Straw Frame

. When Golden Straw paint is dry, carefully paint inside edge of frame with Tompte Red and allow to dry. Spray frame with matte varnish and allow to dry. Following manufacturer's directions, apply antiquing medium, wiping away or adding more to achieve color desired. When thoroughly dry, spray frame with final coat of matte varnish.

. Refer to Meadow Flowers Lap Quilt, making the Small Flower Blocks, page 20 step 1-2. Make one Small Flower Unit to feature in the frame or use a leftover block in the right color palette from another project. Cut a piece of cardboard to fit in the frame and wrap Small Flower Block around the cardboard, securing with tape or a Lacing Stitch (page 95). We chose to place our block off-center for more interest.

. Using photo as reference, use Jewel Glue to adhere beads to Small Flower Block and frame as desired.

Striped Frame

. To paint stripes, use ruler and pencil to mark stripes on frame as desired. Use a new flat brush and Hauser Green Light, Apple Green, and Golden Straw paint. Paint each stripe working with one color at a time and allowing stripes to dry between colors. A narrow piece of red velvet ribbon was glued on later for the red stripe. When stripes are dry, spray frame with matte varnish and allow to dry. Following manufacturer's directions, apply antiquing medium, wiping away or adding more to achieve color desired. When thoroughly dry, spray frame with final coat of matte varnish.

. Glue on narrow red velvet ribbon if desired.

. A piece of gold-colored fabric is featured in the center of the striped frame. Cut a piece of cardboard to fit inside frame then cover with a square of fabric, wrapping ends to the back and securing with tape or a Lacing Stitch (page 95).

. Glue five circle beads and five flower beads to center fabric square.

. Referring to photo for inspiration, tie a green ribbon around frame, adding a circle bead as a buckle. Glue a red bead in the center of circle bead to add more detail and color to the frame.

Hang all three frames as desired.

MEADOW
Luminaries

Bring the vibrant colors of the meadow to your deck or patio with these charming and easy glass lanterns. Tissue paper creates a stained glass effect on inexpensive vases. Beads and appliqués embellish the beautiful colors and designs.

Making the Luminaries

You can't do this wrong! Wrinkles and tears are part of the charm when you make these colorful glass lanterns. Perfect for a late summer party, your kitchen table, or as a hostess gift, these cute glass creations can also be used as a vase or flowerpot.

1. Cut bright colored tissue paper into 1½" - 2" squares or long strips for a striped lantern.

2. Pour some decoupage glue into a throw-away container

3. Starting at the bottom of the vase, spread decoupage glue on lower half of vase.

4. Place tissue squares or strips on glued area, overlapping as desired. Smooth down with brush, applying more decoupage glue and making sure that tissue is totally saturated. Places where two colors of tissue overlap will create a third color. Wrinkles in the tissue just add texture. Have fun with this! You can't do it wrong.

5. Continue applying decoupage and tissue until entire vase is covered. Fold tissue over top edge, overlapping just ¼" and cover with decoupage. Use bristle brush to push tissue into any indentations in the glass. If desired, use decoupage to adhere dried flowers or leaves to vase.

6. Vase will be sticky, so turn it upside down over a glass bottle or set it on another small glass vase to dry. Allow to dry overnight or until all stickiness is gone. If you don't like a section, simply go over it with more tissue paper following same steps as before.

Embellishing the Lanterns

Use tacky glue or jewel glue to adhere small appliqués or beads. Or, string beads onto an elastic string to make a "necklace" for your lantern.

Do not submerge lantern in water! Clean with a damp cloth when needed.

- Vase or Glass Surface
- Tissue Paper or Party Napkins
- Gloss Decoupage Glue
- Inexpensive Bristle Brush
- Optional
    - Glue
    - Assorted Beads
    - Elastic String
    - Dried Flowers or Leaves

Subtle and subdued, seashore-inspired colors
of blue, sand, taupe, and sea green combine for
a restful wave of projects creating a tidepool
of tranquility.

SEASIDE
Serenity

Tidepool Treasures Lap Quilt Finished Size: 50"x 63½"	FIRST CUT		SECOND CUT	
	Number of Strips or Pieces	Dimensions	Number of Pieces	Dimensions
Fabric A Background ⅜ yard each of 3 fabrics	2* 2*	3½ " x 42" 2" x 42" *Cut for each fabric	16*	3½ " squares
Fabric B Accent Squares ¼ yard each of 3 fabrics	2*	3½ " x 42" *Cut for each fabric		
Fabric C Starfish ⅙ yard each of 3 fabrics	2*	2" x 42" *Cut for each fabric		
Fabric D Starfish ⅙ yard each of 3 fabrics	2*	2" x 42" *Cut for each fabric		
Fabric E Centers ⅛ yard each of 3 fabrics	1*	1½ " x 42" *Cut for each fabric	16*	1½ " x 2"
Fabric F Sashing ⅝ yard or 1 yard Fussy Cut	3 1	5½ " x 42" 3½ " x 42"	48 17	5½ " x 2" 3½ " x 2"
Fabric G Sashing ⅓ yard	5	2" x 42"	6 22	2" x 11" 2" x 5"
First Border ⅓ yard	5	2" x 42"		
Second Border ¼ yard	5	1" x 42"		
Outside Border ⅔ yard	6	3½ " x 42"		
Binding ⅝ yard	6	2¾ " x 42"		
Backing - 3⅛ yards Batting - 56" x 69"				

Fabric Requirements and Cutting Instructions

Read all instructions before beginning and use ¼"-wide seam allowance throughout. Read Cutting Strips and Pieces on page 92 prior to cutting fabric.

Getting Started

Colors of life beneath the sea are found in this quilt. Blocks measure 12½" square (unfinished). Each block is made in the same manner, but colors become more intense with the depth of the quilt. Refer to Accurate Seam Allowance on page 92. Whenever possible use the Assembly Line Method on page 92. Press seams in direction of arrows.

Making the Blocks

One design is used to make a total of twelve blocks, four each in three different color ranges using light, medium, and dark fabrics. Use the lightest shades of Fabrics A-E for Block 1.

1. Sew together lengthwise one 2" x 42" Fabric A strip and one 3½" x 42" Fabric B strip. Press seams toward Fabric B. Make two. Cut strip sets into sixteen 3½"-wide segments.

3½

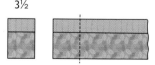

Make 2
Cut 16 segments

2. Sew together lengthwise one 2" x 42" Fabric A strip and one 2" x 42" Fabric D strip. Press seams toward Fabric D. Make two. Cut strip sets into sixteen 5"-wide segments.

5

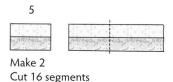

Make 2
Cut 16 segments

Refer to Quick Corner Triangles on page 92. Make a quick corner triangle unit by sewing one 3½" Fabric A square to one unit from step 2 as shown. Press. Make sixteen.

Fabric A = 3½ x 3½
Unit from step 2
Make 16

Sew one unit from step 1 to one unit from step 3 as shown. Press. Make sixteen.

Make 16

Sew one 5½" x 2" Fabric F piece to one 1½" x 2" Fabric E piece as shown. Press. Make sixteen. Sew this unit to one unit from step 4 as shown. Press. Make sixteen.

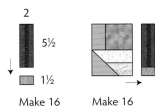

2

5½

1½

Make 16   Make 16

Sew two units from step 5 together as shown. Press. Make eight. Sew two of these units together as shown. Refer to Twisting Seams on page 92. Press. Make four and label Block 1. Block measures 12½" square.

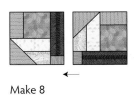

Make 8

Block 1

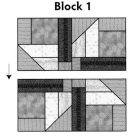

Make 4
Block measures 12½" square

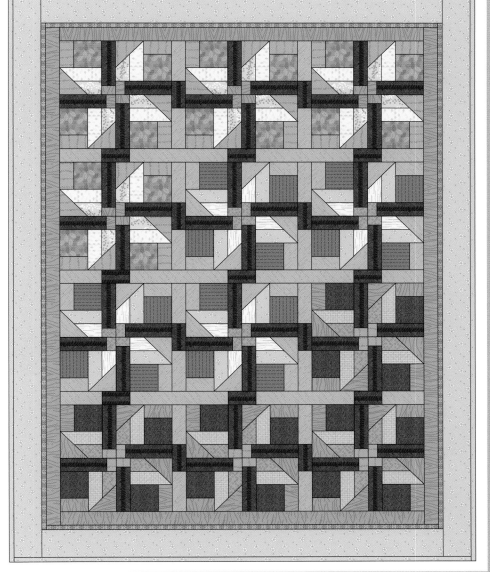

Tidepool Treasures
Lap Quilt
Finished Size: 50" x 63½"

A beach bounty inspired lap quilt creates a serene scene when draped on a couch or folded at the edge of a bed. Starfish blocks are caught in a net of rich chocolate fabric in this soothing seascape.

7. Refer to photo on page 27, layout on page 29, and steps 1-6 to make four medium shaded blocks (label Block 2) and four dark shaded blocks (label Block 3). Blocks measures 12½" square.

Block 2

Block 3

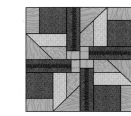

Make 4
Block measures 12½" square

Make 4
Block measures 12½" square

8. Sew one 3½" x 2" Fabric F piece between two 2" x 5" Fabric G pieces as shown. Press. Make eight and label Unit 1.

Unit 1

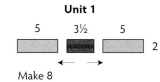

5	3½	5	

Make 8

9. Sew together two 2" x 5" Fabric G pieces, three 3½" x 2" Fabric F pieces, and two 2" x 11" Fabric G pieces as shown. Press. Make three and label Unit 2.

Unit 2

| 5 | 3½ | 11 | 3½ | 11 | 3½ | 5 | 2 |

Make 3

Assembly

1. Referring to photo on page 27 and layout on page 29, sew together three of Block 1 and two of Unit 1. Press seams toward Unit 1 and label Row 1.

2. Referring to photo on page 27 and layout on page 29, sew together one of Block 1, two of Block 2, and two of Unit 1. Press and label Row 2.

3. Referring to photo on page 27 and layout on page 29, sew together two of Block 2, one of Block 3, and two of Unit 1. Press and label Row 3.

4. Referring to photo on page 27 and layout on page 29, sew together three of Block 3 and two of Unit 1. Press and label Row 4.

5. Referring to photo on page 27 and layout on page 29, sew together rows from steps 1-4 and three of Unit 2, checking orientation of rows prior to sewing. Press seam toward Unit 2.

6. Referring to Adding the Borders on page 94, sew 2" x 42" First Border strips together end-to-end to make one continuous 2"-wide First Border strip. Measure quilt through center from side to side. Cut two 2"-wide First Border strips to this measurement. Sew to top and bottom of quilt. Press seams toward border.

7. Measure quilt through center from top to bottom including border just added. Cut two 2"-wide First Border strips to this measurement. Sew to sides of quilt. Press.

8. Refer to steps 1 and 2 to join, measure, trim, and sew 1"-wide Second Border and 3½"-wide Outside Border strips to top, bottom, and sides of quilt. Press.

Layering and Finishing

1. Cut backing crosswise into two equal pieces. Sew pieces together lengthwise to make one 56" x 80" (approximate) backing piece. Press and trim to 56" x 69".

2. Referring to Layering the Quilt on page 94, arrange and baste backing, batting, and top together. Hand or machine quilt as desired.

3. Refer to Binding the Quilt on page 94. Sew 2¾" x 42" binding strips end-to-end to make one continuous 2¾"-wide binding strip. Bind quilt to finish.

Decorating with
SEA SHELLS

A simple shell combines with decorative papers and beads in a shadow box to create a serene wall piece. Craft chalk adds shading to the deckle edge of a sea blue paper and a piece of faux fan coral creates a textured backdrop for the shell. A variety of sea-colored beads cluster in the shell. Clear glue holds everything in place.

SEA SHELL
Planter

Like shells uncovered by the tide on a white sand beach, this handsome planter will show off all your favorite plants. Or, get a double dose of seashore memories by displaying large shells, rocks, and driftwood in the planter.

Making the Planter

1. Using the features of planter as a guide, decide on placement of each element.

2. Refer to Cutting Glass on page 95. Cut green glass, if needed, for planter rim.

3. Following manufacturer's directions, spread mastic on one side of planter. Working quickly, press shells and glass gems into mastic, creating the desired design.

4. Apply mastic to another section and repeat process until sides are covered with shells/gems.

5. Apply mastic to rim of planter and place green glass into mastic. Clean off any excess mastic and allow to dry 48 hours.

6. Using a putty knife, spread grout into all spaces between decorative elements.

7. Wearing gloves, use sponge to wipe off excess grout. Wipe flat across the surface and rinse and wring sponge thoroughly after each pass. Make sure that tops of all shells are exposed and spaces in between are covered with grout.

8. When excess grout is removed, use a soft cloth (rinsing often) to carefully clear the top of each gem, shell, and glass piece of grout.

9. Mist the surface several times as the grout cures to avoid cracking. Allow to dry for several days.

10. If grout didn't include a sealer, apply a grout sealer according to manufacturer's directions.

Note: Excess moisture can damage planter. Line planter with plastic before placing plants.

SUPPLIES

- Terracotta Planter
- Assorted Sea Shells
- Glass Gems in Ocean Blue
- Green Colored Glass
- Tile Mastic
- Putty Knife or Mastic Spreader
- Pre-Mixed Grout*- Sanded White
- Grout Sponge
- Glass Cutter
- Lubrication Oil
- Glass Pliers
- Safety Goggles
- Latex or Rubber Gloves
- Soft Cloth Rag

*Look for a pre-mixed grout that includes a sealer; or purchase grout sealer separately. It is important that sanded grout be used for this project as spaces between mosaic items will be wider than for a standard mosaic.
Read Mosaic Safety Precautions on page 95 before beginning this project.

SEA to Shore

Sea to Shore Bed Quilt Finished Size: 77" x 91"	FIRST CUT		SECOND CUT	
	Number of Strips or Pieces	Dimensions	Number of Pieces	Dimensions
Fabric A Beginning Square ¼ yard	2	3½" x 42"	20	3½" square
Fabric B Block 1st Border ⅓ yard	5	1½" x 42"	20 20	1½" x 4½" 1½" x 3½"
Fabric C Block 2nd Border ½ yard	6	2½" x 42"	20 20	2½" x 6½" 2½" x 4½"
Fabric D Block 3rd Border ½ yard	8	1½" x 42"	20 20	1½" x 7½" 1½" x 6½"
Fabric E Block 4th Border ½ yard	9	1½" x 42"	20 20	1½" x 8½" 1½" x 7½"
Fabric F Block 5th Border ½ yard	10	1½" x 42"	20 20	1½" x 9½" 1½" x 8½"
Fabric G Block 6th Border 1 yard	12	2½" x 42"	20 20	2½" x 11½" 2½" x 9½"
Fabric H Block 7th Border ⅔ yard	14	1½" x 42"	20 20	1½" x 12½" 1½" x 11½"
Fabric I Block 1 Border ¾ yard	9	2½" x 42"	10 10	2½" x 14½" 2½" x 12½"
Fabric J Block 2 Border ¾ yard	9	2½" x 42"	10 10	2½" x 14½" 2½" x 12½"
First Border ⅜ yard	7	1½" x 42"		
Second Border ½ yard	8	1½" x 42"		
Third Border 1⅓ yards	8	5½" x 42"		
Fourth Border ½ yard	9	1½" x 42"		
Outside Border ¾ yard	9	2½" x 42"		
Binding ⅞ yard	10	2¾" x 42"		
Backing - 7⅛ yards		Batting - 85" x 99"		

Fabric Requirements and Cutting Instructions

Read all instructions before beginning and use ¼"-wide seam allowance throughout. Read Cutting Strips and Pieces on page 92 prior to cutting fabric.

Getting Started

Ocean waves lapping the shoreline are reflected in this easy-to-construct quilt. One block with two different outside borders measure 14½" square (unfinished). Blocks are set to reveal the rippling effect of the ocean. Refer to Accurate Seam Allowance on page 92. Whenever possible use the Assembly Line Method on page 92. Press seams in the direction of arrows.

Making the Blocks

1. Sew one 1½" x 3½" Fabric B piece to one 3½" Fabric A square as shown. Press. Sew this unit to one 1¼" x 4½" Fabric B piece as shown. Press. Make twenty.

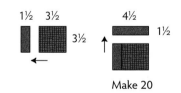

Make 20

2. Sew one 2½" x 4½" Fabric C piece to one unit from step 1 as shown. Press. Sew this unit to one 2½" x 6½" Fabric C piece as shown. Press. Make twenty.

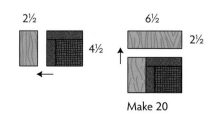

Make 20

3. Sew one 1½" x 6½" Fabric D piece to one unit from step 2 as shown. Press. Sew this unit to one 1½" x 7½" Fabric D piece. Press. Make twenty.

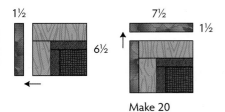

1½

6½

7½

1½

Make 20

4. Sew one 1½" x 7½" Fabric E piece to one unit from step 3 as shown. Press. Sew this unit to one 1½" x 8½" Fabric E piece. Press. Make twenty.

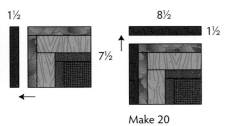

1½

7½

8½

1½

Make 20

5. Sew one 1½" x 8½" Fabric F piece to one unit from step 4 as shown. Press. Sew this unit to one 1½" x 9½" Fabric F piece. Press. Make twenty.

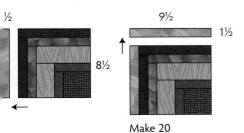

½

8½

9½

1½

Make 20

Sea to Shore Bed Quilt

Finished Size: 77" x 91"

6. Sew one 2½" x 9½" Fabric G strip to one unit from step 5 as shown. Press. Sew this unit to one 2½" x 11½" Fabric G strip. Press. Make twenty.

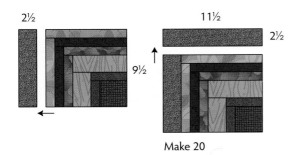

2½

9½

11½

2½

Make 20

7. Sew one 1½" x 11½" Fabric H strip to one unit from step 6 as shown. Press. Sew this unit to one 1½" x 12½" Fabric H strip. Press. Make twenty.

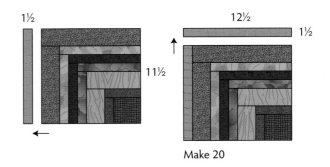

1½

11½

12½

1½

Make 20

Sea to Shore
Bed Quilt

Finished Size: 77" x 91"

Waves of easy blocks flow
together to create a serene sea of
soft color on this bed quilt.

8. Sew one 2½" x 12½" Fabric I strip to one unit from step 7 as shown. Press. Make ten. Sew this unit to one 2½" x 14½" Fabric I strip. Press. Make ten. Label Block 1. Block measures 14½" square.

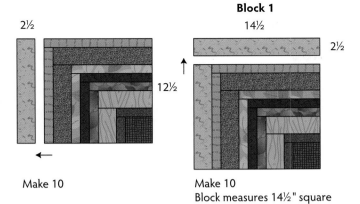

Block 1

2½

14½

12½

2½

Make 10

Make 10
Block measures 14½" square

9. Sew one 2½" x 12½" Fabric J strip to one unit from step 7 as shown. Press. Make ten. Sew this unit to one 2½" x 14½" Fabric J strip. Press. Make ten. Label Block 2. Block measures 14½" square.

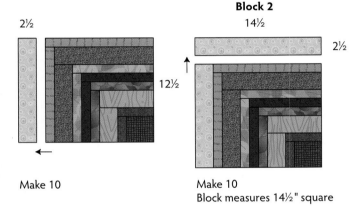

Block 2

2½

14½

12½

2½

Make 10

Make 10
Block measures 14½" square

10. Referring to photo on page 33 and layout, arrange and sew together five rows of four blocks each, two of each variation, alternating Block 1 and 2 placement from row to row. Press seams in opposite directions from row to row.

Adding the Borders

1. Referring to Adding the Borders on page 94, sew 1½" x 42" First Border strips together end-to-end to make one continuous 1½"-wide First Border strip. Measure quilt through center from side to side. Cut two 1½"-wide First Border strips to this measurement. Sew to top and bottom of quilt. Press seams toward border.

2. Measure quilt through center from top to bottom including borders just added. Cut two 1½"-wide First Border strips to this measurement. Sew to sides of quilt. Press.

3. Refer to steps 1 and 2 to join, measure, trim, and sew 1½"-wide Second Border, 5½"-wide Third Border, 1½"-wide Fourth Border and 2½"-wide Outside Border strips to top, bottom, and sides of quilt. Press.

Layering and Finishing

1. Cut backing crosswise into three equal pieces. Sew pieces together lengthwise to make one 85" x 120" (approximate) backing piece. Press and trim to 85" x 99".

2. Referring to Layering the Quilt on page 94, arrange and baste backing, batting, and top together. Hand or machine quilt as desired.

3. Refer to Binding the Quilt on page 94. Sew 2¾" x 42" binding strips end-to-end to make one continuous 2¾"-wide binding strip. Bind quilt to finish.

Sea Shell
CANDLESTICK

A chipped wooden candlestick is reclaimed as a seaside accessory with an easy painting technique and the addition of shells.

Sand candlestick and prime with white gesso. Allow to dry thoroughly before coating with Americana® Antique White Acrylic Paint. Several coats may be needed for good coverage. When completely dry, apply a brown antiquing medium following manufacturer's directions. Use hot glue to adhere shells to candlestick as desired.

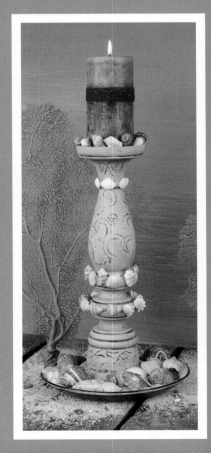

Earthy hues of ivory, moss, misty blue, paprika, black, and brown add drama and depth to a rock fall of easy projects that capture nature's subtler tones.

ROCKY
Revelations

ROCK Slide

Rock Slide Lap Quilt Finished Size: 58"x 67½"	FIRST CUT		SECOND CUT	
	Number of Strips or Pieces	Dimensions	Number of Pieces	Dimensions
Fabrics A-1, A-2, A-3 ⅛ yard each of 3 fabrics	1*	2" x 42" *Cut for each fabric	10*	2" squares
Fabric B ⅓ yard	6	1½" x 42"	2 10 10 10 8	1½" x 10" 1½" x 8" 1½" x 6" 1½" x 4" 1½" x 2"
Fabrics C & K ⅓ yard each of 2 fabrics	5*	1½" x 42" *Cut for each fabric	6* 6* 6* 6*	1½" x 10" 1½" x 8" 1½" x 6" 1½" x 4"
Fabrics D, M & P ⅓ yard each of 3 fabrics	5*	1½" x 42" *Cut for each fabric	4* 6* 6* 6* 2*	1½" x 10" 1½" x 8" 1½" x 6" 1½" x 4" 1½" x 2"
Fabric E ⅜ yard	7	1½" x 42"	8 8 8 8	1½" x 10" 1½" x 8" 1½" x 6" 1½" x 4"
Fabrics F, N & U ⅙ yard each of 3 fabrics	2*	1½" x 42" *Cut for each fabric	4* 4* 4* 4*	1½" x 8" 1½" x 6" 1½" x 4" 1½" x 2"
Fabrics G, Q & S ⅓ yard each of 3 fabrics	6*	1½" x 42" *Cut for each fabric	4* 8* 8* 8* 4*	1½" x 10" 1½" x 8" 1½" x 6" 1½" x 4" 1½" x 2"
Fabric H ¼ yard	3	1½" x 42"	4 4 4 4	1½" x 10" 1½" x 8" 1½" x 6" 1½" x 4"
Fabrics I, L & R ¼ yard each of 3 fabrics	4*	1½" x 42" *Cut for each fabric	2* 6* 6* 6* 4*	1½" x 10" 1½" x 8" 1½" x 6" 1½" x 4" 1½" x 2"
Fabrics J & O ⅛ yard each of 2 fabrics	1*	1½" x 42" *Cut for each fabric	2* 2* 2* 2*	1½" x 8" 1½" x 6" 1½" x 4" 1½" x 2"
Fabric T ⅓ yard	6	1½" x 42"	4 10 10 10 6	1½" x 10" 1½" x 8" 1½" x 6" 1½" x 4" 1½" x 2"
First Border ¼ yard	6	1" x 42"		
Second Border ⅜ yard	6	1¾" x 42"		
Outside Border ¾ yard	7	3½" x 42"		
Binding ⅝ yard	7	2¾" x 42"		
Backing - 3⅝ yards		Batting - 64" x 73½"		

Fabric Requirements and Cutting Instructions

Read all instructions before beginning and use ¼"-wide seam allowances throughout. Read Cutting Strips and Pieces on page 92 prior to cutting fabric.

Getting Started

Close examinations of rock formations reveal many shades of colors: gray, blue, green, brown, and black. These subtle shades are incorporated into a traditional Courthouse Steps block to make our quilt. Blocks and rows are sewn together with like fabrics to form larger fabric units or color patches. For ease of construction, label all fabrics prior to cutting. Place cut pieces in labeled resealable bags. Blocks measure 10" square (unfinished). Refer to Accurate Seam Allowance on page 92. Whenever possible use the Assembly Line Method on page 92. Press seams in direction of arrows.

Making the Blocks

1. Sew one 2" Fabric A-1 square between one 1½" x 2" Fabric P piece and one 1½" x 2" Fabric S piece as shown. Press. Make two.

   Make 2

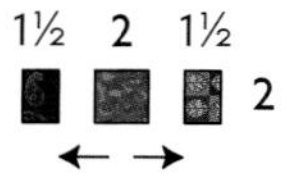

2. Sew one unit from step 1 between one 1½" x 4" Fabric B piece and one 1½" x 4" Fabric T piece as shown. Press. Make two.

   Make 2

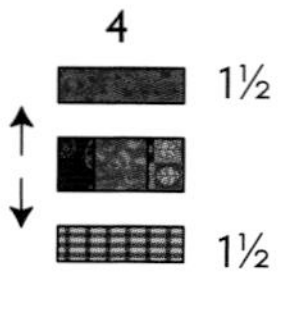

3. Sew one unit from step 2 between one 1½" x 4" Fabric P piece and one 1½" x 4" Fabric S piece as shown. Press. Make two.

   Make 2

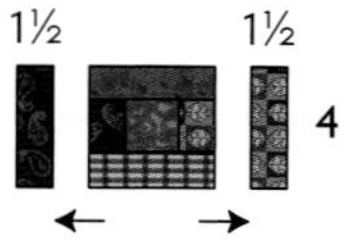

4. Sew one unit from step 3 between one 1½" x 6" Fabric B piece and one 1½" x 6" Fabric T piece as shown. Press. Make two.

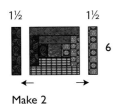

6

1½

1½

Make 2

5. Sew one unit from step 4 between one 1½" x 6" Fabric P piece and one 1½" x 6" Fabric S piece as shown. Press. Make two.

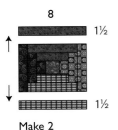

1½   1½

6

Make 2

6. Sew one unit from step 5 between one 1½" x 8" Fabric B piece and one 1½" x 8" Fabric T piece as shown. Press. Make two.

8

1½

1½

Make 2

7. Sew one unit from step 6 between one 1½" x 8" Fabric P piece and one 1½" x 8" Fabric S piece as shown. Press. Make two.

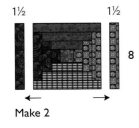

1½   1½

8

Make 2

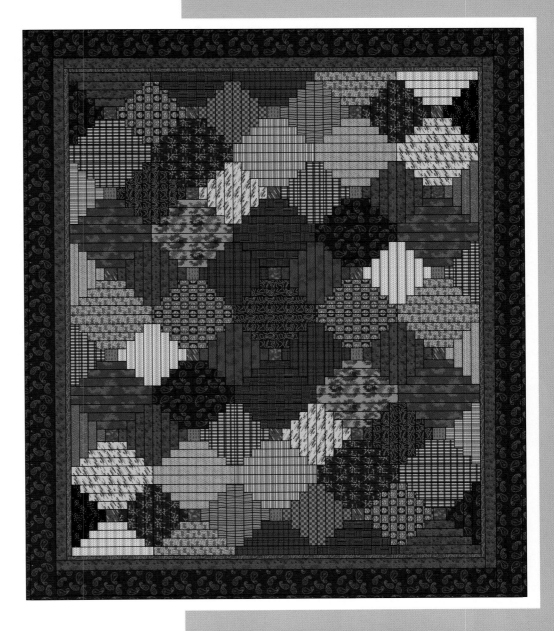

Rock Slide
Lap Quilt
Finished Size: 58" x 67½"

The traditional structure of Courthouse Steps blocks creates a mesmerizing mirage of color, shape, and texture on this warm and welcoming lap quilt.

8. Sew one unit from step 7 between one 1½" x 10" Fabric B piece and one 1½" x 10" Fabric T piece as shown. Press. Make two.

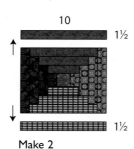

10

1½

1½

Make 2

Re-press seams in opposite direction on some blocks as needed for row construction.

9. Refer to steps 1-8 and diagram below to construct blocks. Fabrics are listed in the following order: Center/Left Side/Right Side/Top/Bottom. Make two blocks each using the following fabric combinations: A-2/S/N/K/Q, A-3/N/F/R/D, A-1/F/Q/C/M, and A-2/Q/J/I/G. Arrange and sew together five blocks, one of each combination, as shown. Press. Make two rows.

Fabrics are listed below as follows
Center/Left Side/Right Side/Top/Bottom

A-1/P/S/B/T   A-2/S/N/K/Q   A-3/N/F/R/D   A-1/F/Q/C/M   A-2/Q/J/I/G

Make 2

10. Refer to steps 1-8 and diagram below to make two blocks in each of the following fabric combinations: A-3/D/L/T/E, A-1/L/G/Q/H, A-2/G/T/D/K, A-3/T/B/M/P, and A-1/B/O/G/E. Arrange and sew together five blocks, one of each combination, as shown. Press. Make two rows.

A-3/D/L/T/E   A-1/L/G/Q/H   A-2/G/T/D/K   A-3/T/B/M/P   A-1/B/O/G/E

Make 2

11. Refer to steps 1-8 and diagram below to make two blocks each of the following fabric combinations: A-2/M/B/E/C, A-3/B/R/H/S, A-1/R/U/K/L, A-2/U/I/P/S, and A-3/I/T/E/C. Arrange and sew together five blocks, one of each block combination, as shown. Press. Make two rows.

A-2/M/B/E/C   A-3/B/R/H/S   A-1/R/U/K/L   A-2/U/I/P/S   A-3/I/T/E/C

Make 2

12. Referring to photo on page 37 and layout on page 39, arrange and sew rows from steps 9, 10 and 11 together. Make two. Sew these two units together, rotating second row to match Fabric C, S, and L sections in center of quilt. Press.

Adding the Borders

1. Sew 1" x 42" First Border strips together end-to-end to make one continuous 1"-wide First Border strip. Referring to Adding the Borders on page 94, measure quilt through center from side to side. Cut two 1"-wide First Border strips to this measurement. Sew to top and bottom of quilt. Press seams toward border.

2. Measure quilt through center from top to bottom including border just added. Cut two 1"-wide First Border strips to this measurement. Sew to sides of quilt. Press.

3. Refer to steps 1 and 2 to join, measure, trim, and sew 1¾"-wide Second Border strips and 3½"-wide Outside Border strips to top, bottom, and sides of quilt. Press.

Layering and Finishing

1. Cut backing crosswise into two equal pieces. Sew pieces together lengthwise to make one 65" x 80" (approximate) backing piece. Press.

2. Referring to Layering the Quilt on page 94, arrange and baste backing, batting, and top together. Hand or machine quilt as desired.

3. Referring to Binding the Quilt on page 94, sew 2¾" x 42" binding strips end-to-end to make one continuous 2¾"-wide binding strip. Bind quilt to finish.

Decorating with
ROCKS

Easy to find, rocks make fun decorating accessories! Look on the beach or along a creek or river bed for water-rounded rocks. Chunks of slate also work well when decorating with rocks*. Or, check local craft stores for bags of rocks.

Rock Frame

Show off your outdoor adventure pictures in a rock-topped frame. Use hot glue to adhere rocks to an unfinished wooden frame. Spray paint with the color of your choice for a unique and handsome accessory. Use a sea sponge and acrylic craft paint to add dark shading if desired.

Word Rocks

Create an organic and unusual display for coffee table or buffet by grouping a variety of rocks and votive candles on a tray. Just for fun, use press-on or rub-on scrapbook letters to add words to a few of the rocks.

Sticks n' Stones

The simplicity and serenity of nature are showcased in this quiet composition of a few beautiful rocks, sticks, and moss. Look for a shadowbox frame that enables you to put a mat next to the glass before inserting your natural items. Simply use hot glue to attach a piece of grass cloth to the shadowbox's wooden backing, then glue rocks and twigs to the grass cloth. Insert into the shadowbox and attach according to shadowbox directions.

*Always check regulations in State and National Parks before gathering any natural items.

ROCKY Reach

Tote Bag

Rocky Reach Tote Bag Finished Size: approximately 14"x 14½"	FIRST CUT	
	Number of Strips or Pieces	Dimensions
Fabric A Background ½ yard	1 1	14¾" square Triangle from template
Fabric B Accent Stripes ⅙ yard each of 4 fabrics	1* *Cut for each fabric	3" x 24"
Fabric C Accent Squares Scraps each of 10 fabrics	1* *Cut for each fabric	3" squares
Fabric D Top Accent Border & Closure Loop ⅛ yard	2 1	1¼" x 14¾" ½" x 8¼"
Handle ⅛ yard	1	3" x 27½"
Lining ½ yard	2	14¾" x 15¼"
Fusible or Sew-in Interfacing - ½ yard Buttons - 4 Perlé Cotton or Embroidery Floss		

Fabric Requirements and Cutting Instructions

Read all instructions before beginning and use ¼"-wide seam allowances throughout. Read Cutting Strips and Pieces on page 92 prior to cutting fabric.

Getting Started

Add a splash of style to your fall wardrobe with this luscious wool tote bag. Refer to Accurate Seam Allowance on page 92. Press all seams open to reduce bulk for this project.

Felting the Wool

Refer to Tips for Felting Wool on page 95 to prepare wool fabrics. Extra yardage was provided in our cutting chart since wool could shrink up to 30%.

Making the Tote

Optional: Pressing wool will flatten texture obtained when felting. For this project we elected to use iron on interfacing and press all seams open. Option: To maintain the texture obtained from felting wool use non-fusible interfacing, baste in place, and finger press all seams.

1. Refer to diagram below to make triangle template. Draw a 15½" x 7¾" rectangle on paper, tagboard, or cardstock. Mark center of one long side of rectangle. Draw a line from corner to center of long side. Repeat for opposite corner. Cut out large triangle for template.

Triangle Template

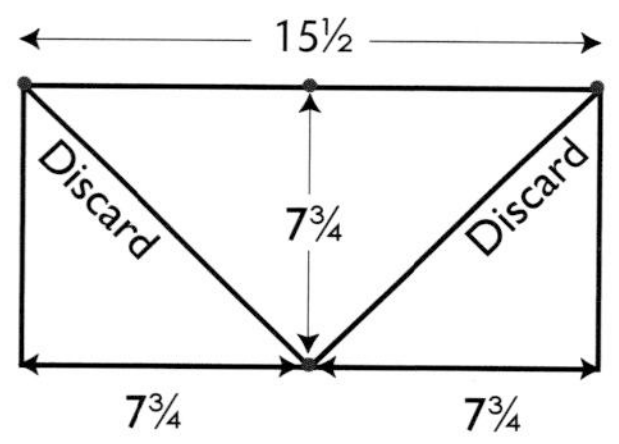

2. Sew ten assorted 3" Fabric C squares together to make four rows as shown: single square, two squares, three squares, and four squares. Press seams open. Sew rows together, aligning right sides as shown. Press. Place interfacing on wrong side of unit: press or stitch in place following manufacturer's directions. Trim interfacing to match wool unit.

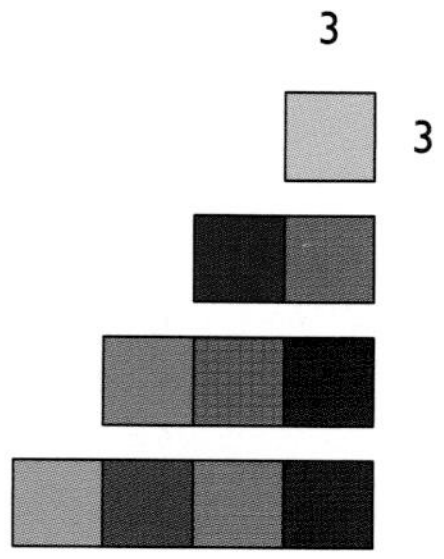

Place triangle template from step 1 on unit from step 2 as shown. Using removable fabric marker, draw a line across top. This is a placement line only; **do not trim.**

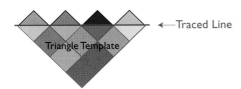

←—Traced Line

Triangle Template

Sew four 3" x 24" assorted Fabric B strips together as shown. Press. Place triangle template's short sides along outside edges or unit. Cut triangles from strip set as shown. Press or baste interfacing to wrong side of smaller triangle units following manufacturer's directions. Baste along outside long edge, and trim interfacing to match units.

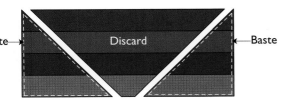

ste→ Discard ←—Baste

Baste Interfacing to wrong side of triangle units.

Using triangle template from step 1, cut one triangle from Fabric A piece. Press. Press or baste interfacing to wrong side of unit following manufacturer's directions. Trim interfacing to match unit.

Sew units from steps 3, 4, and 5 together as shown. Press seams. Align one 1¼" x 14¾" Fabric D strip along top of unit's drawn line, stitch in place, and trim to remove excess fabric. Press.

Top

. Refer to photo, and Embroidery Stitch Guide on page 93 to stitch, a Primitive Stitch along accent squares seam lines.

. Sew one 1¼" x 14¾" Fabric D strip to 14¾" Fabric A square. Press.

. Place units from steps 7 and 8 right sides together. Using ¼"-wide seam, sew around sides and bottom of tote leaving top edge free of stitching. Turn right side out and press.

0. Press or stitch interfacing to wrong side of 3" x 27½" Handle piece. Fold under ¼" along one long side of Handle piece. Place opposite long side of Handle piece under folded edge and press. Topstitch along folded edges to make handle. Add any additional stitches as desired.

Rocky Reach
Tote Bag
Finished Size: approximately 14" x 14½"

The deep colors and rich texture of wool provide a firm foundation for this handy and handsome tote bag. Hand-stitching and buttons add handmade details.

11. With right sides together, place handle ends, at side seams of bag. Baste ends in place. Pin handle in this position away from top edge as shown for the following steps.

12. Fold ½" x 8¼" Fabric D piece in half crosswise to form a loop, pin to center back of upper edge of bag, matching raw edges. Baste ends in place keeping loop in this position for the following steps.

13. Place two 14¾" x 15¼" Lining pieces right sides together. Using ¼"-wide seam, sew along bottom edge and sides as shown, leaving top 14¾" edge free of stitches and one 5" opening along one side edge for turning.

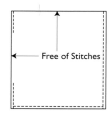

Free of Stitches

14. Place units from step 12 and 13 right sides together making sure handle and closure loop are between these layers. Using ¼"-wide seam, sew around top edges. Stitch again approximately ⅛" from previous stitches toward seam allowance. Clip corners and turn right side out through lining side opening. Hand-stitch opening closed. Place lining in bag, press and stitch in-the-ditch between tote and top accent border.

15. Referring to photo on page 43, stitch buttons to tote.

Rocky Reach Tote Bag
Finished Size: approximately 14" x 14½"

CELL PHONE
Carrier

SUPPLIES

- **Body—Wool scrap**
  One 4" x 10" piece
- **Top Accent—Wool scrap**
  One 2" x 7½" piece
  One 2" square
- **Lining—Scrap**
  One 4" x 10" piece
- **Strap—Wool scrap**
  One 2" x 9" piece
- **Iron-on Interfacing—Scrap**
  One 1¾" x 8¾" piece
- **Button**
- **Perlé Cotton**
- **Optional:** Wool Scrap for Initial

Making the Cell Phone Carrier

Measure your cell phone or iPod and adjust measurements as needed. Our PDA measured 4½" x 2¼" and ¾" deep. Read all instructions before beginning and use ¼"-wide seam allowances throughout.

1. Fold 4" x 10" Body piece crosswise right sides together and stitch sides using ¼"-wide seam allowance. Press. Repeat step to sew 4" x 10" lining piece side seams.

2. Turn case right side out and place lining inside case unit, wrong sides together. Matching top raw edges, baste in place.

3. Fold 2" x 7½" Top Accent piece crosswise right sides together, aligning raw edges, stitch 2" sides together to form a loop.

4. Place accent piece right sides together with lining piece, aligning raw edges. Hand baste ¼" from top edge.

5. Fold accent strip to right side, covering basting stitch. Edge-stitch in place, approximately ⅛" from edge.

6. If desired, select an approximately 1½" high initial and trace a reverse image on paper side of lightweight fusible web. Use appropriate fabric to prepare appliqué for fusing. Fuse appliqué to 2" accent square. Add decorative stitches as desired.

7. Referring to photo, stitch unit from step 6 to case as desired.

8. Following manufacturer's instructions, fuse 1¾" x 8¾" Interfacing piece to 2" x 9" Strap piece. Fold piece in half lengthwise. Referring to Embroidery Stitch Guide on page 93 and using a Blanket Stitch, stitch raw edges together.

9. Referring to photo, attach one end of strap piece to back of case stitching a large "X". Bring strap to front and secure in place with a button.

10. Refer to manufacturer's instructions to sew magnetic closure to case.

ROCKY
Accessories

Create wonderful and useful accessories for your Rocky Reach Tote Bag with leftover wool. A charming clutch and monogrammed cell phone holder make this tote ensemble absolutely terrific.

WOOL
Clutch

Making the Clutch

Read all instructions before beginning and use ¼"-wide seam allowances throughout.

1. Referring to manufacturer's instructions, fuse 8¾" x 9¾" interfacing piece to wrong side of 9" x 10" Clutch piece.

2. Sew together strips of assorted wool scraps large enough to cut one 2½" x 9" piece for clutch flap.

3. Place flap piece from step 2 right sides together with 9" x 10" Clutch piece, stitch using ¼"-wide seam along one 9" edge. Press seam open.

4. Place lining right sides together with unit from step 3. Stitch around all sides leaving a 4" opening for turning. Zigzag or serge seams if desired. Clip corners, turn right side out, and press. Hand stitch opening closed.

5. Stitch-in-the-ditch at seam between flap and clutch and top stitch ¼" from bottom edge.

6. Fold clutch with lining right sides together. Place bottom edge just below flap and pin sides in place. Referring to Embroidery Guide on page 93, use a Blind Stitch to hand-stitch sides in place. Add additional stitches near flap for extra strength.

7. Sew buttons to flap and add decorative stitches as desired. Follow manufacturer's directions to attach magnetic closure to clutch.

SUPPLIES

- Clutch—⅓ yard Wool
  One 9" x 10" piece
- Clutch Flap—Assorted wool scraps
- Clutch Lining—⅓ yard
  One 9" x 11½" piece
- Iron-on Interfacing—¼ yard
  One 8¾" x 9¾" piece
- Magnetic Snap Closure
- Buttons—2
- Perlé Cotton

The velvety rich tones of rain-drenched earth and woods illuminated with sparks of copper and gold sunshine create a soul-satisfying palette in our forest grouping.

FOREST Foliage

FOREST Fantasy

Bed Quilt

Making the Block

Forest Fantasy Bed Quilt Finished Size: 58¾" x 70"	FIRST CUT		SECOND CUT	
	Number of Strips or Pieces	Dimensions	Number of Pieces	Dimensions
Fabric A Background 3¼ yards	2	12⅝" x 42"	6	12⅝" squares* *cut twice diagonally
	7	5" x 42"	49	5" squares
	20	2½" x 42"		
Fabric B Triangles & Squares ¼ yard each of 20 fabrics	2	5" squares (Cut 2 from 11 fabrics)		
	3	5" squares (Cut from 9 fabrics)		
	1**	2½" x 42" **Cut for each fabric		
Outside Border ⅓ yard	7	1¼" x 42"		
Binding ⅝ yard	7	2¾" x 42"		
Backing - 3⅝ yards Batting - 65" x 76"				

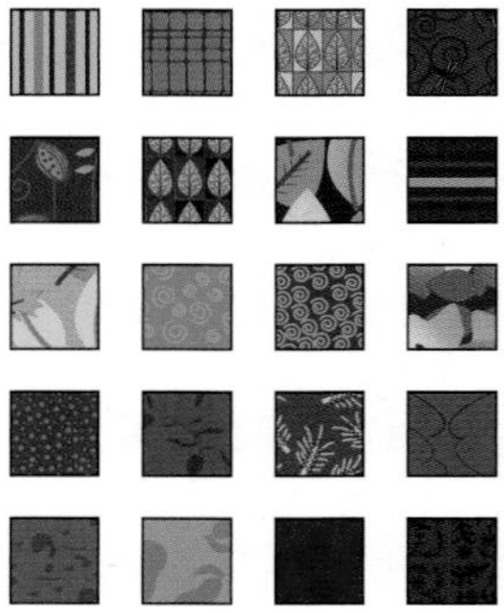

Fabric Requirements and Cutting Instructions

Read all instructions before beginning and use ¼"-wide seam allowances throughout. Read Cutting Strips and Pieces on page 92 prior to cutting fabric.

Getting Started

Rich tones of trees and earth and easy block construction create a quilt depicting the serenity of the forest. Blocks measure 8½" square (unfinished). Refer to Accurate Seam Allowance on page 92. Whenever possible use the Assembly Line Method on page 92. Press seams in direction of arrows.

1. Sew together lengthwise one 2½" x 42" Fabric A strip and one 2½" x 42" Fabric B strip. Press seams toward Fabric A. Make twenty, one of each combination. Cut strip sets into one hundred ninety-six 2½"-wide segments. Cut nine or ten of each combination to obtain the number needed.

2½

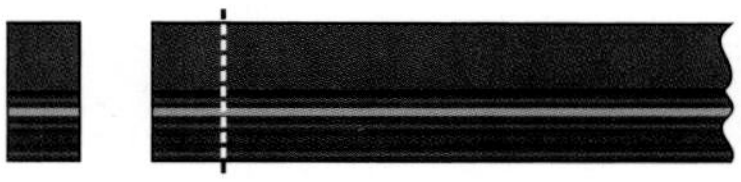

Make 20
(1 of each combination)
Cut 196 segments

2. Sew together two different units from step 1 alternating Fabric A placement as shown. Refer to Twisting Seams on page 92. Press. Make ninety-eight.

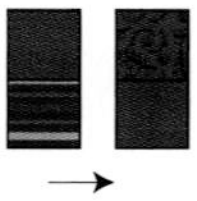

Make 98

3. Draw a diagonal line on wrong side of one 5" Fabric B square. Place marked square and one 5" Fabric A square right sides together. Sew scant ¼" away from drawn line on **both** sides to make half-square triangles as shown. Make forty-nine. Cut **on** drawn line and press. Square to 4 ½". This will make ninety-eight half-square triangle units.

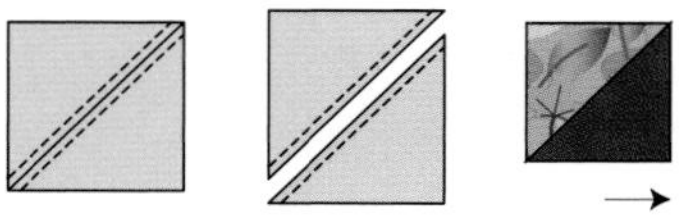

B = 5 x 5
A = 5 x 5
Make 49
(From assorted fabrics)

Square to 4½
Make 98
Half-square triangles

4. Sew one unit from step 3 to one unit from step 2 as shown checking orientation of blocks prior to sewing. Press. Make ninety-eight. Sew pairs together as shown. Twist seams. Press. Make forty-nine. Block measures 8½" square.

Make 98

Make 49
Block measures
8½" square

5. Sew two Fabric A triangles together as shown. Press. Make two and label Rows 1 and 11.

Make 2
Label Row 1 & 11

6. When sewing, place triangle pieces next to the feed dogs to minimize stretching of bias edges. Noting orientation of blocks, sew together two Fabric A triangles and two blocks from step 4 as shown. Press. Make two and label Rows 2 and 10.

Make 2
Label Rows 2 & 10

7. Sew together two Fabric A triangles and four blocks as shown. Press. Make two and label Rows 3 and 9.

Make 2
Label Rows 3 & 9

Forest Fantasy
Bed Quilt
Finished Size: 58¾" x 70"

Layers of greens and browns sparked with earth-warming copper and gold create the dense foliage of a rain forest in this handsome quilt. Strip piecing and half square triangles make quick work of the repeating block and the full spectrum of nature's colors combine to achieve a sense of peacefulness and tranquility.

8. Sew together two Fabric A triangles and six blocks as shown. Press. Make two and label Rows 4 and 8.

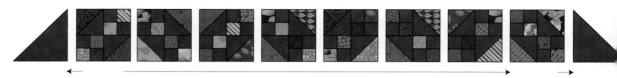

Make 2
Label Rows 4 & 8

9. Sew together two Fabric A triangles and eight blocks as shown. Press. Make two and label Rows 5 and 7.

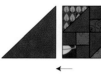

Make 2
Label Rows 5 & 7

10. Sew together two Fabric A triangles and nine blocks as shown. Press and label Row 6.

Label Row 6

11. Referring to photo on page 47 and layout on page 49, arrange and sew rows 1-11 together. Press.

Adding the Borders

1. Sew 1¼" x 42" Outside Border strips together end-to-end to make one continuous 1¼"-wide Outside Border strip. Referring to Adding the Borders on page 94, measure quilt through center from side to side. Cut two 1¼"-wide Outside Border strips to this measurement. Sew to top and bottom of quilt. Press seams toward border.

2. Measure quilt through center from top to bottom including border just added. Cut two 1¼"-wide Outside Border strips to this measurement. Sew to sides of quilt. Press.

Layering and Finishing

1. Cut backing crosswise into two equal pieces. Sew pieces together lengthwise to make one 65" x 80" (approximate) backing piece.

2. Referring to Layering the Quilt on page 94, arrange and baste backing, batting, and top together. Hand or machine quilt as desired.

3. Referring to Binding the Quilt on page 94, sew 2¾" x 42" binding strips end-to-end to make one continuous 2¾"-wide binding strip. Bind quilt to finish.

Nature Lover's Banner (page 52)
Leaf Appliqué
Make 6

Tracing Line _____

FOREST
Findings

Nature provides all kinds of decorations on the forest floor. Pinecones, acorns, twigs, seeds, moss, and rocks are just a few of nature's gifts.*

Fill a glass vase with all your forest finds for an eye-catching and organic centerpiece. Place the vase on a round from a birch tree for added interest. Small birch branches, moss-covered twigs, slate, pinecones, and acorns all reflect the forest's bounty. For even greater impact, group the vase with a candle or use two or three vases in various sizes.

Create a striking frame for a beautiful forest photo with twigs. Perfect for the den or a cabin, this frame uses landscaping cuttings to create a picture prefect presentation. Simply remove all leaves from cuttings and allow twigs to dry thoroughly. Paint an unfinished wooden frame the same color as the twigs to serve as a base. Using sisal or string, tie bundles of twigs to the frame, securing in every direction as shown.

Trim string as needed. Since ties go around the wooden frame, photo mat may need to be notched in each corner so mat fits snugly in the frame.

*Always check regulations in State and National Parks before gathering any natural items.

NATURE Lover's Banner

Nature Lover's Banner Finished Size: 30" x 26½"	FIRST CUT		SECOND CUT	
	Number of Strips or Pieces	Dimensions	Number of Pieces	Dimensions
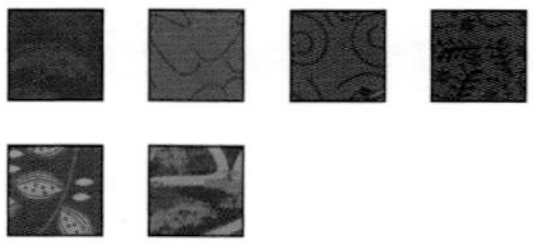 **Fabric A** Appliqué Background **scrap** each of 6 fabrics	1*	5½" x 7½" *Cut for each fabric		
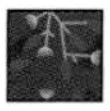 **Fabric B** Stripes & Decorative Leaf Edge ½ yard	2 12	3" x 42" Leaf Edge	6	3" x 13"
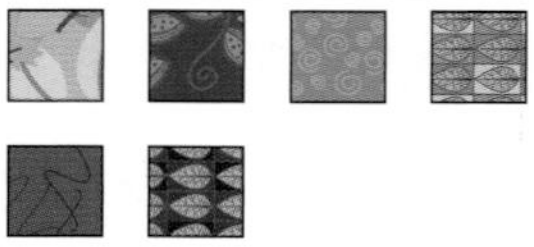 **Fabric C** Stripes, Tabs & Decorative Leaf Edge ¼ yard each of 6 fabrics	1* 1* 12	5½" x 3½" 3" x 13" Leaf Edge *Cut for each fabric		
Fabric D Accent Border ⅛ yard	1	1¼" x 42"	1	1¼" x 30½"
Fabric E Accent Border ⅙ yard	2	1¾" x 42"	2	1¾" x 30½"

Leaf Appliqués - Assorted wool scraps	Batting - 34" x 26"
Letter Appliqués - ⅛ yard	Lightweight Fusible Web - ⅝ yard
Backing - ⅞ yard	Beads & Buttons (Optional)

Fabric Requirements and Cutting Instructions

Read all instructions before beginning and use ¼"-wide seam allowances throughout. Read Cutting Strips and Pieces on page 92 prior to cutting fabric.

Getting Started

Wool appliqué leaves spell out "NATURE" while cotton stripes and pieces bring the colors of the forest to our banner.

Refer to Accurate Seam Allowance on page 92. Whenever possible use the Assembly Line Method on page 92. Press seams in direction of arrows.

Making the Banner

1. Arrange and sew together six different 5½" x 7½" Fabric A pieces as shown. Press.

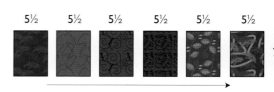

2. Arrange and sew together lengthwise six 3" x 13" Fabric B strips and six assorted 3" x 13" Fabric C strips as shown. Press. Cut strip set into one 10½" x 30½" piece and one 1¾" x 30½" piece.

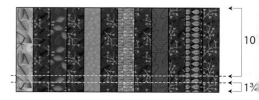

3. Sew unit from step 1 between 1¾" x 30½" strip set from step 2 and 1¼" x 30½" Fabric D strip. Press.

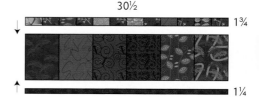

4. Sew unit from step 3 between two 1¾" x 30½" Fabric E strips. Press.

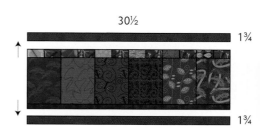

5. Referring to layout on page 54 and photo, sew 10½" x 30½" strip set from step 2 to bottom of unit from step 4, checking orientation of strip set fabrics prior to sewing. Press.

Adding the Appliqués

Refer to appliqué instructions on page 93. Our instructions are for Quick-Fuse Appliqué, but if you prefer hand appliqué, reverse templates and add ¼"-wide seam allowances.

. Use Leaf Appliqué Pattern on pages 50 and "NATURE" pattern on page 54 to trace leaves and letters on paper side of fusible web. Use appropriate wool or cotton fabrics to prepare all appliqués for fusing.

. Fuse one appliqué letter to each leaf to spell "NATURE".

. Refer to layout on page 54 and photo to position and fuse appliqués to quilt. Finish appliqué edges with machine satin stitch or other decorative stitching as desired.

Layering and Finishing

. Fold one 5½" x 3½" Fabric C piece crosswise right sides together. Sew using ¼"-wide seam along 3½" side. Turn right side out. Press, placing seam in center back. Make six, one of each Fabric C piece for quilt tabs.

. Fold quilt tabs from step 1 in half crosswise. Referring to photo, align tabs along top edge of quilt matching raw edges, folded edge in towards center, and matching fabric placement with strip set unit. Baste in place.

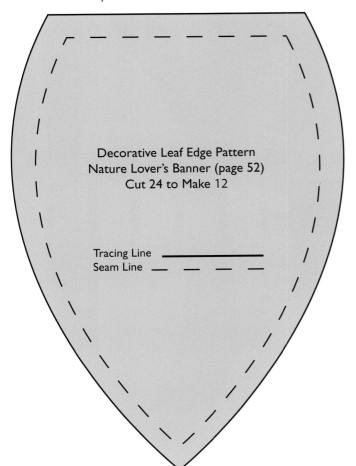

Decorative Leaf Edge Pattern
Nature Lover's Banner (page 52)
Cut 24 to Make 12

Tracing Line ——————
Seam Line — — — —

Nature Lover's
Banner
Finished Size: 30" x 26½"

Nature's Beauty - misty rain on pine trees, mossy creek beds, a blanket of fallen leaves - is celebrated in this simple, sensual, wall quilt. Bars of color flow through the banner from top to bottom for a uniquely satisfying design.

Meadow Luminaries
(page 24)

3. Using Decorative Leaf Edge Pattern on page 53 cut twelve leaf shapes from assorted Fabric C pieces, two of each combination and twelve Fabric B pieces. Place matching pairs right sides together, sew using a ¼"-wide seam allowance leaving top edge free of stitches. Clip curves and turn right side out. Press. Make twelve.

4. Arrange decorative leaves along bottom edge of quilt, right sides together, aligning raw edges. Baste in place.

5. Layer and center banner and backing right sides together, making sure tabs and decorative leaf edge are in between layers, place on batting, wrong side of backing on batting. Using ¼"-wide seam, stitch around all edges, leaving a 6" opening on one side for turning. Trim batting close to stitching and backing even with banner edges. Clip corners, turn, and press. Hand-stitch opening closed. Press tabs and decorative leaf edge away from center.

6. Machine or hand quilt as desired. Add beads, buttons, and other embellishments as desired.

Nature Lover's Banner Letter Appliqués

Patterns are reversed for use with Quick-Fuse Appliqué (page 93)

Tracing Line _____

Nature Lover's Banner
Finished Size: 30" x 26½"

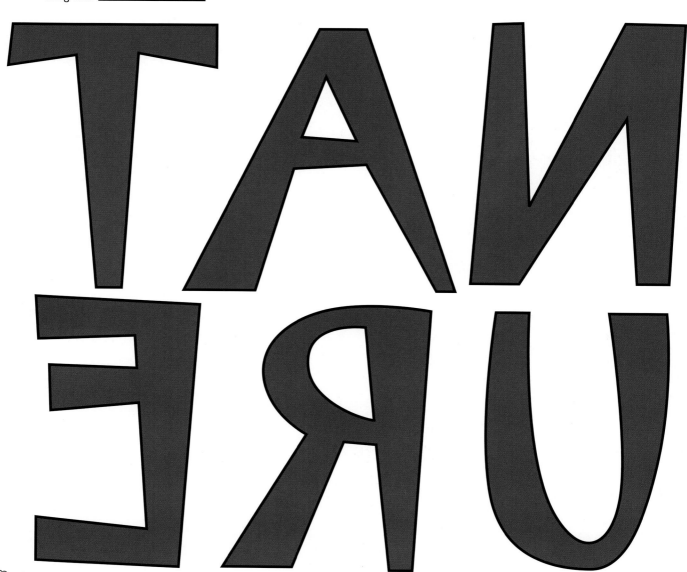

LIGHT
in the Forest

Light up a forest-inspired room with this woodsy candleholder. We reused scrap materials for an earth-friendly project.

Read all instructions before beginning.

1. Follow all standard safety practices when using power tools. Using a table saw, trim 14" 4" x 4" board at a 15° angle on all sides so that sides taper. If a lip like the one shown is desired, set table saw to leave ⅜" at top edge.

2. Using glass votive holder as your template, measure and mark placement for five votive holders on top of board. Using power drill and hole saw bit in a size slightly larger than votive holders, drill holes at places marked, sinking holes ½". Use chisel and hammer to clear wood from center of drilled hole. We recommend testing hole size and depth on a piece of scrap lumber before drilling into prepared board. Make sure that glass votive holder will fit into drilled hole and depth is pleasing before drilling on prepared board.

3. Sand as needed to smooth rough spots. Since this candleholder is rustic, fine sanding isn't necessary.

4. Apply Folk Art® Antiquing Medium or walnut stain to candleholder with paint brush. Use a cloth to wipe off any excess stain or medium. Allow to dry thoroughly.

5. Plan leaf design. We used five different leaf stamps, the largest is about 3½" square. Using a paintbrush spread a combination of raw sienna and antique white paint on raised surface of one stamp. Carefully place stamp in position on side of wooden candleholder and pat gently. Lift straight up being careful not to smudge paint. Repeat process to stamp all leaves desired, being careful not to overlap on any wet paint. Allow to dry, then repeat for other sides and ends if desired. Allow to dry thoroughly.

6. Using fine sandpaper, sand stamped leaves to eliminate high points and mute color. Remove sanding debris with damp cloth or tack cloth.

7. Mix a small amount of burnt umber paint with clear glaze. A ratio of 1 part paint to 3 parts glaze works well. Spread glaze over entire candleholder, wiping off or adding more as needed until desired tone is achieved. Allow to dry.

8. Spray candleholder with one or two coats of matte varnish to protect color.

9. Attach metal or wood legs as desired.

10. Place votive candles in glass holders and place in candleholder holes. Use florist clay to level votive holders if needed.

Candleholder

- **14" Piece of 4" x 4" Lumber**
- **Metal Stand** (Optional) – Recycle a plant stand, candleholder or other "found" metal piece
- **Five Glass Votive Holders**
- **Five Votive Candles**
- **Large Leaf Rubber Stamps**
- **Acrylic Craft Paint** – Delta Ceramcoat® Raw Sienna, Burnt Umber, and Americana® Antique White
- **Walnut Wood Stain or Antiquing Medium**
- **Clear Glaze**
- **Matte Spray Varnish**
- **Power Drill with Hole Saw Bit**
- **Chisel and Hammer**
- **Table Saw**
- **Sandpaper**
- **Assorted Paintbrushes**

SUPPLIES

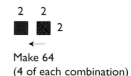
Forest Table Runner Finished Size: 13" x 53"	FIRST CUT		SECOND CUT	
	Number of Strips or Pieces	Dimensions	Number of Pieces	Dimensions
Fabric A Background ⅝ yard	2	4" x 42"	16	4" squares
	1	2½" x 42"	2	2½" x 12½"
	4	2" x 42"	64	2" squares
Fabric B Square & Triangles ⅙ yard each of 16 fabrics	1*	4" square		
	4*	2" squares		
		*Cut for each fabric		
Binding ⅜ yard	4	2¾" x 42"		
Backing - 1 yard Batting - 57" x 17"				

Fabric Requirements and Cutting Instructions

Read all instructions before beginning and use ¼"-wide seam allowances throughout. Read Cutting Strips and Pieces on page 92 prior to cutting fabric.

Getting Started

Crisp cool days bring an ever-changing play of colors to forest trees and ground cover. Our easy to make table runner can be constructed from colorful scraps from previous projects or yardage as noted on our cutting chart. Blocks measure 12½" square (unfinished). Refer to Accurate Seam Allowance on page 92. Whenever possible use the Assembly Line Method on page 92. Press seams in direction of arrows.

Making the Block

1. Sew one 2" Fabric A square to one 2" Fabric B square. Press. Make sixty-four, four of each combination.

Make 64
(4 of each combination)

2. Sew together two different units from step 1 as shown, alternating Fabric A placement. Refer to Twisting Seams on page 92. Press. Make thirty-two.

Make 32

3. Draw a diagonal line on wrong side of one 4" Fabric B square. Place marked square and one 4" Fabric A square right sides together. Sew scant ¼" away from drawn line on **both** sides to make half-square triangles as shown. Make sixteen. Cut **on** drawn line and press. Square to 3½". This will make thirty-two half-square triangle units.

B = 4 x 4
A = 4 x 4
Make 16
(From assorted fabrics)

Square to 3½"
Make 32
Half-square triangles

4. Sew one unit from step 3 to one unit from step 2 as shown noting orientation of Fabric A. Press. Make thirty-two.

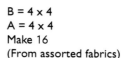

Make 32

Sew two units from step 4 together as shown, checking Fabric A placement prior to sewing. Twist seams. Press. Make sixteen.

Make 16

Sew two units from step 5 together as shown. Press. Make eight.

Make 8

Sew two units from step 6 together as shown. Twist seams. Press. Make four. Block measures 12½" square.

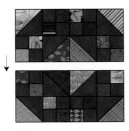

Make 4
Block measures 12½" square

Referring to photo, arrange and sew together four blocks from step 7. Press. Sew this unit between two 2½" x 12½" Fabric A strips. Press seams toward Fabric A.

Layering and Finishing

Cut backing crosswise into two equal pieces. Sew pieces together lengthwise to make one 18" x 80" (approximate) backing piece. Press and trim to 18" x 57".

Referring to Layering the Quilt on page 94, arrange and baste backing, batting, and top together. Hand or machine quilt as desired.

Referring to Binding the Quilt on page 94, sew 2¾" x 42" binding strips end-to-end to make one continuous 2¾"-wide binding strip. Bind quilt to finish.

Blur the boundaries between the natural world and your home with this velvety-hued table runner. Perfect for autumn celebrations, this table runner brings the peace and tranquility of the forest to your home.

Forest Table Runner
Finished Size: 13" x 53"

The vibrant colors of mountains at twilight glow in classic quilt designs where color placement creates peaks and valleys. Plum, magenta, deep blue, garnet, and tan make a striking and sophisticated statement in this group of projects.

MOUNTAIN
Masterpiece

MOUNTAIN Peak

Mountain Peak Lap Quilt Finished Size: 48½" x 48½"	FIRST CUT		SECOND CUT	
	Number of Strips or Pieces	Dimensions	Number of Pieces	Dimensions
Fabric A Center Border Background ⅜ yard	3	3½" x 42"	24	3½" squares
Fabric B Outside Border Background ¾ yard	7	3½" x 42"	72	3½" squares
Fabric C Large & Small Triangles ⅓ yard each of 12 fabrics	1* 8*	8½" x 42" 3½" squares *Cut for each fabric	2*	8½" squares
Binding ⅝ yard	6	2¾" x 42"		
Backing - 3 yards Batting - 54" x 54"				

Fabric Requirements and Cutting Instructions

Read all instructions before beginning and use ¼"-wide seam allowances throughout. Read Cutting Strips and Pieces on page 92 prior to cutting fabric.

Getting Started

Twilight stretches over our mountain peaks to reflect the deep reds, blues, purples, and browns of nature. This quilt uses half-square triangles to make Delectable Mountain blocks for the center panel and Flying Geese units for the border. The center panel measures 23" square (unfinished) and the Flying Geese Border units measure 3" x 5½" (unfinished). Refer to Accurate Seam Allowance on page 92. Whenever possible use the Assembly Line Method on page 92. Press seams in direction of arrows.

Making the Center Panel

Extra units are made in steps 1-2 to allow for the arrangement of fabric to obtain a "scrappy" look to this quilt. It is recommended to lay out all units prior to sewing steps 3-7.

1. Draw a diagonal line on wrong side of one 8½" Fabric C square. Place marked square and one 8½" Fabric C square right sides together. Sew scant ¼" away from drawn line on **both** sides to make half-square triangles as shown. Make twelve from assorted fabric. Cut **on** drawn line and press. Square to 8". This will make twenty-four half-square triangle units; twenty will be used for this project.

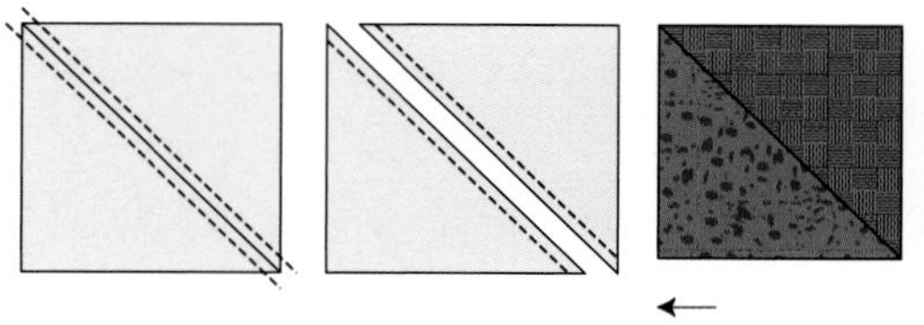

C = 8½ x 8½
C = 8½ x 8½
Make 12
(assorted fabrics)

←
Square to 8"
Make 24
Half-square triangles
(This project uses 2...)

2. Draw a diagonal line on wrong side of one 3½" Fabric A square. Place marked square and one 3½" Fabric C square right sides together. Sew scant ¼" away from drawn line on **both** sides to make half-square triangles as shown. Make twenty-four, two of each combination. Cut **on** drawn line and press. Square to 3". This will make forty-eight half-square triangle units; forty-five will be used for the Center Border.

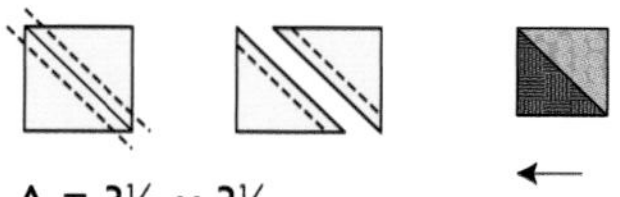

A = 3½ x 3½
C = 3½ x 3½
Make 24
(2 of each combination)

←
Square to 3"
Make 48
Half-square triangles
(Center Border uses 45)

Sew three units from step 2 together as shown. Press. Make six. Sew together three of these units and two units from step 1 as shown. Press. Make two.

Make 6

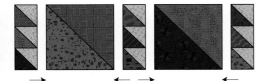

Make 2

Arrange and sew together nine units from step 2 as shown. Press. Make three.

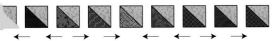

ake 3

Referring to photo on page 59 and layout, sew together three units from step 4 and two units from step 3. Press. Center panel measures 23" square.

Pay close attention to the rotation of the units in this step and step 7 prior to sewing. Referring to photo on page 59 and layout, sew together three units from step 1. Press. Make four. Sew two of these units to top and bottom of center panel from step 5.

Referring to photo on page 59 and layout, sew one unit from step 6 between two units from step 1. Press. Make two and sew to sides of quilt. Press.

Mountain Peak
Lap Quilt
Finished Size: 48½" x 48½"

Shadows and sunshine, peaks and valleys emerge from mountains of lovely color on this classic quilt. Traditional Delectable Mountain blocks combine with Flying Geese for a quilt with natural appeal.

Making the Flying Geese Border

Extra units are made in step 1 to obtain a "scrappy" look in this quilt. In steps 2 and 3, use one unit with the fabric pressed toward Fabric B and one unit pressed toward Fabric C to form pairs.

1. Draw a diagonal line on wrong side of one 3½" Fabric B square. Place marked square and one 3½" Fabric C square right sides together. Sew scant ¼" away from drawn line on **both** sides to make half-square triangles as shown. Make seventy-two, six of each combination. Cut **on** drawn line and press half as shown and half in the opposite direction. Square to 3". This will make one hundred forty-four half-square triangle units; one hundred thirty-six will be used in the outside border units.

B = 3½ x 3½
C = 3½ x 3½
Make 72
(6 of each combination)

← Square to 3"
Make 144
Half-square triangles
(Outside Border uses 136)

2. Arrange and sew four units from step 1 together as shown. Refer to Twisting Seams on page 92. Press. Make four corner units.

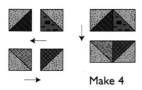

Make 4

3. Sew two units from step 1 together as shown. Press. Make sixty, pressing half in the opposite direction.

Make 60

4. Referring to layout on page 61 and photo, arrange and sew together fifteen units from step 3. Press. Make four.

5. Referring to layout on page 61 and photo, sew two units from step 4 to top and bottom of quilt. Press.

6. Sew one unit from step 4 between two corner units from step 2. Press. Make two. Sew to sides of quilt Press.

Mountain Peak Lap Quilt
Finished Size: 48½" x 48½"

Layering and Finishing

1. Cut backing crosswise into two equal pieces. Sew pieces together lengthwise to make one 54" x 80" (approximate) backing piece. Press and trim to 54" x 54".

2. Referring to Layering the Quilt on page 94, arrange and baste backing, batting, and top together. Hand or machine quilt as desired.

3. Refer to Binding the Quilt on page 94. Sew 2¾" x 42" binding strips end-to-end to make one continuous 2¾"-wide binding strip. Bind quilt to finish.

Mountain Pillow - Optional Pillow B and Mountain Welcome Banner

Tracing Line _____

Quarter Moon Pattern
(¼ of 6" circle)

For 6" circle, align straight edges
and trace four times to complete circle.

MOUNTAIN Pillows

Getting Started

Read all instructions before beginning and use ¼"-wide seam allowances throughout. Refer to Quick-Fuse Appliqué instructions on page 93 for quarter-moon appliqués.

Making Pillow A - 12" square finished

Refer to Mountain Peak Quilt, Step 1, Page 60. Use four 8" half-square triangle leftover units squared to 4½", or four 5" Fabric A squares, to make four half-square triangle units, squared to 4½".

Referring to layout, sew four 4½" half-square triangle units from Step 1, to make pillow top. Refer to Twisting Seams on page 92. Press.

Sew unit from step 2 between two 2½" x 8½" Fabric B strips. Press.

Sew unit from step 3 between two 2½" x 12½" Fabric B strips. Press.

Refer to Finishing Pillows on page 95, step 1, to prepare pillow top for quilting. Quilt as desired. Embellish with buttons if desired.

Use two 9½" x 12½" Backing pieces and refer to Finishing Pillows, page 95, steps 2-4 to sew backing.

Insert 12" pillow form **OR** refer to Pillow Forms on page 95 to make pillow form if desired.

Making Pillow B - 15" square finished

1. Refer to Mountain Peak Quilt, Step 1, page 60. Use four 8" half-square triangle units, squared to 7" or use four 7½" Fabric A squares to make four half-square triangle units squared to 7".

2. Refer to photo, arrange and sew four half-square units together to form pillow top.

OPTIONAL: Trace four Quarter Moon Patterns on page 62, onto fusible web and fuse to wrong side of Fabric C. Cut circle into fourths and fuse one quarter circle to each corner of pillow. Finish rounded edges with decorative stitching as desired.

3. Sew unit from step 2 between two 1½" x 13½" Fabric B strips. Press.

4. Sew unit from step 3 between two 1½" x 15½" Fabric B strips. Press.

5. Refer to Finishing Pillows on page 95, step 1, to prepare pillow top for quilting. Quilt as desired. Embellish with buttons if desired.

6. Use two 10½" x 15½" Backing pieces and refer to Finishing Pillows, page 95, steps 2-4 to sew backing.

7. Insert 15" pillow form **OR** refer to Pillow Forms on page 95 to make pillow form if desired.

Pillow B (Option)   Pillow A   Pillow B

Mountain Welcome Banner Finished Size: 17" x 37½"	FIRST CUT		SECOND CUT	
	Number of Strips or Pieces	Dimensions	Number of Pieces	Dimensions
Fabric A Background & Bottom Binding ½ yard	1	12½" x 42"	1 1 1 1	12½" square 4½" x 14½" 2¾" x 16½" Binding 2" x 14½"
Fabric B Light Triangles Scraps each of 4 fabrics	2*	4½" squares *Cut for each fabric		
Fabric C Dark Triangles Scraps each of 4 fabrics	2*	4½" squares *Cut for each fabric		
Fabric D Accent Borders ⅛ yard	1	1½" x 42"	1 1	1½" x 14½" 1½" x 12½"
Fabric E Accent Borders ⅛ yard	2	1½" x 42"	2 1	1½" x 14½" 1½" x 12½"
Fabric F Prairie Points ⅙ yard each of 2 fabrics	3*	4" squares *Cut for each fabric		
Fabric G Prairie Points Scrap	2	4" squares		
Outside Border & Binding ½ yard	3 1 2	2¾" x 42" Binding 2½" x 42" 1½" x 42"	1 2	2½" x 14½" 1½" x 37"
Backing - ⅝ yard Batting - 20" x 41" Mountain Appliqué - ⅜ yard Moon Appliqué - Scrap Lightweight Fusible Web - ½ yard				

Fabric Requirements and Cutting Instructions

Read all instructions before beginning and use ¼"-wide seam allowances throughout. Read Cutting Strips and Pieces on page 92 prior to cutting fabric.

Getting Started

As the full moon reveals the silhouette of a distant mountain, colors of nature are reflected in the moonlight. Refer to Accurate Seam Allowance on page 92. Whenever possible use the Assembly Line Method on page 92. Press seams in direction of arrows.

Making the Banner

Refer to appliqué instructions on page 93. Our instructions are for Quick-Fuse Appliqué, but if you prefer hand appliqué, add ¼"-wide seam allowance.

1. On paper side of fusible web draw a 9½" x 12½" rectangle. Measure and mark center top as shown. Mark sides 1¾" from each bottom corner as shown. Draw a line from side marks to center top to make mountain pattern. Cut around traced piece approximately ¼" outside of traced lines. Following manufacturer's instructions, press large triangular shpaed fusible web to wrong side of Mountain Appliqué fabric. Cut on drawn lines.

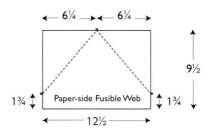

2. Refer to Quarter Moon Pattern on page 6? to create 6" circle and trace it to paper side of fusible web. Use appropriate fabric to prepare circle appliqué for fusing.

Refer to photo on page 66 and layout to position and fuse appliqués to 12½" Fabric A square. Finish appliqué edges with machine satin stitch or other decorative stitching as desired.

Sew 1½" x 12½" Fabric E strip to top of unit from step 3 and 1½" x 12½" Fabric D strip to bottom. Press seams towards accent strips. Sew this unit between two 1½" x 14½" Fabric E strips as shown. Press.

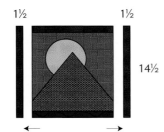

Draw a diagonal line on wrong side of one 4½" Fabric B square. Place marked square and one 4½" Fabric C square right sides together. Sew scant ¼" away from drawn line on **both** sides to make half-square triangles as shown. Make eight, two of each combination. Cut **on** drawn line and press. Square to 4". This will make sixteen half-square triangle units, four of each combination.

Fabric B = 4½ x 4½   Square to 4"
Fabric C = 4½ x 4½   Make 16
Make 8   Half-square triangles
(2 of each combination) (4 of each combination)

Refer to photo on page 66 and layout to arrange units from step 5 in rows. Sew four units from step 5 together as shown to make a row. Press. Make four rows, each using a different combination of units. Press alternating rows in opposite directions.

Make 4
(each using a different combination)

Sew rows from step 6 together as shown. Press. Referring to photo on page 66 and layout, sew this unit to bottom of unit from step 4. Press.

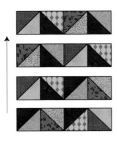

Mountain
Welcome Banner
Finished Size: 17" x 37½"

The moon rises behind the mountain casting snippets of moonlight on the valley below—for such a small piece, this banner tells an ageless story in striking colors. On your door or on the wall, this banner will evoke a serene scene.

8. Fold and press one 4" Fabric F square in half diagonally, wrong sides together. Fold and press diagonally in half again, as shown, to make one Prairie Point. Raw edges will be together. Make six, three of each color. Repeat step using two 4" Fabric G squares. Make two.

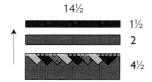

Make 8
(3 each of Fabric F
and 2 of Fabric G)

9. Arrange and baste eight Prairie Points along top edge of 4½" x 14½" Fabric A strip, overlapping and matching raw edges as shown. Baste in place. Sew 2" x 14½" Fabric A strip between 1½" x 14½" Fabric D strip and Prairie Point unit as shown. Press.

14½
1½
2
4½

10. Referring to layout on page 65 and photo, sew unit from step 7 between 2½" x 14½" Outside Border Strip and unit from step 9. Press.

11. Sew two 1½" x 37" Outside Border strips to sides of unit from step 10. Press.

Layering and Finishing

1. Referring to Layering the Quilt on page 94, arrange and baste backing, batting, and top together. Hand or machine quilt as desired.

2. Refer to Binding the Quilt on page 94 and bind quilt to finish. Note: we used 2¾" x 16½" Fabric A strip for bottom binding and 2¾"-wide binding strips for top and side binding.

Mountain Welcome Banner
Finished Size: 17" x 37½"

MOUNTAIN
Placemats

Mountain Placemat Finished Size: approximately: 15" x 19" FOR ONE PLACEMAT	OPTION 1		OPTION 2	
	Number of Strips or Pieces	Dimensions	Number of Strips or Pieces	Dimensions
Fabric A Center Background ½ yard	1	11" x 14½"		
Fabric B Light Triangles Scraps each of 4 fabrics			2*	4½" squares *Cut for each fabric
Fabric C Dark Triangles Scraps each of 4 fabrics			2*	4½" squares *Cut for each fabric
Fabric D Accent ⅛ yard	2	1½" x 14½"	2	1½" x 14½"
Fabric E Border ¼ yard	2 2	2" x 14½" 1" x 16"	2 2	2" x 14½" 1" x 16"
Fabric F Prairie Points ⅛ yard each of 2 fabrics	6*	4" squares *Cut for each fabric	6*	4" squares *Cut for each fabric
Fabric G Prairie Points ⅛ yard	4	4" squares	4	4" squares
	Backing - ½ yard Batting - 16" x 20"		Backing - ½ yard Batting - 16" x 20"	

Getting Started

Instructions are for one Mountain Placemat. Adjust yardage and cuts for quantity desired. Read all instructions before beginning and use ¼"-wide seam allowances throughout. Read cutting Strips and Pieces on page 92 prior to cutting fabric.

Making One Placemat

1. **Option 1** - 11" x 14½" (solid center): skip to step 2.
   Option 2 - (pieced center): follow step 5 in Making Banner on page 65 to make twelve 4" Fabric B and C half-square triangle units. Referring to step 2 diagram arrange and sew four rows with three blocks each. Press.

2. Arrange and sew together two 2" x 14½" Fabric E strips, two 1½" x 14½" Fabric D strips, and 11" x 14½" Fabric A piece or unit from step 1 as shown. Press.

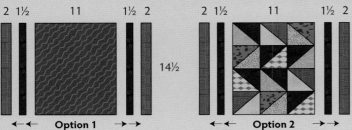

Option 1	Option 2

3. Sew two 1" x 16" Fabric E strips to top and bottom of placemat as shown. Press.

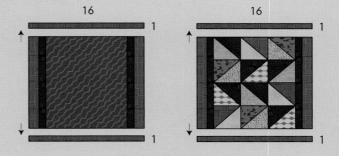

4. Follow step 8 in Making Welcome Banner on page 66 to make sixteen Prairie Points.

5. Arrange and baste eight Prairie Points along each outside edge of placemat, overlapping and matching raw edges as shown. Baste in place. Keep prairie points in this position for layering the placemat.

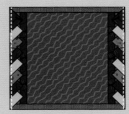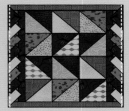

Layering and Finishing

1. Trim backing to 17" x 18". Layer and center placemat top and backing right sides together on batting (wrong side of backing on batting). Using ¼"-wide seam, stitch around placemat edges, leaving a 4" opening on one side for turning. Trim batting close to stitching and backing even with placemat edges. Clip corners, turn, and press. Hand-stitch opening closed.

2. Machine or hand quilt as desired.

Option 1

Option 2

Vivid hues will enliven any room with
the colors of a flower garden.
Yellow, garnet, crimson, purple, and leafy green
are a brilliant combination in
an eye-catching garden of projects.

FLORAL
Flamboyance

Flamboyant FLOWER Wall Quilt

Flamboyant Flower Wall Quilt Finished Size: 21½" x 42½"	FIRST CUT		SECOND CUT	
	Number of Strips or Pieces	Dimensions	Number of Pieces	Dimensions
Fabric A Appliqué Background ⅜ yard	1	10½" x 42"	3	10½" squares
Fabric B Background & Border ¾ yard	1	11½" x 42"	2	11½" x 4¾"
			1	11½" x 4¼"
			1	11½" x 2¼"
			2	11½" x 1¾"
	4	2½" x 42" (3 for border)	2	2½" x 17"
	1	1¾" x 17"	2	1¾" x 17"
	1	1½" x 42"	2	1½" x 17"
Fabric C Block Accent ⅙ yard	4	1" x 42"	6	1" x 11½"
			6	1" x 10½"
Fabric D Mock Piping ⅛ yard	3	1" x 42"	2	1" x 38"
			2	1" x 17"
Binding ⅜ yard	4	2¾" x 42"		

Backing - 1⅓ yards

Batting - 25" x 46"

Appliqués - Assorted scraps

Lightweight Fusible Web - 1 yard

Assorted Beads - (Optional)

Fabric Requirements and Cutting Instructions

Read all instructions before beginning and use ¼"-wide seam allowances throughout. Read Cutting Strips and Pieces on page 92 prior to cutting fabric.

Getting Started

These dramatic flowers add flamboyance, excitement, and style to any room setting. To make a bolder statement, flowers were extended beyond the edges of Fabric A squares, fused, and then trimmed, creating the effect of flowers bursting from the center of each block. Refer to Accurate Seam Allowance on page 92. Whenever possible use the Assembly Line Method on page 92. Press seams in direction of arrows.

Adding the Appliqués

Refer to appliqué instructions on page 93. Our instructions are for Quick-Fuse Appliqué, but if you prefer hand appliqué, reverse templates and add ¼"-wide seam allowances.

1. Use Flamboyant Flowers #1, #2 and #3 patterns on pages 72-75 to trace flowers and leaves on paper side of fusible web. Use appropriate fabrics to prepare all appliqués for fusing. **Tip:** To reduce bulk, cut away center of fusible web, ½" inside traced line before fusing to appliqué fabrics.

2. Refer to photo on page 69 and layout to position and fuse Flower #1 appliqués to one 10½" Fabric A square. **Note:** We used an appliqué-pressing sheet (page 93) to fuse elements together to make a unit, and again when fusing units to background since some elements extend beyond the outside edges. Trim excess appliqué fabric even with square. Repeat to fuse and trim Flowers #2 and #3 to 10½" Fabric A squares. Finish appliqué edges with machine satin stitch or other decorative stitching as desired.

Making the Wall Quilt

1. Sew Flower #1 unit between two 1" x 10½" Fabric C pieces. Press toward Fabric C. Sew this unit between two 1" x 11½" Fabric C pieces as shown. Press. Make three, one of each flower variation.

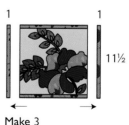

Make 3
(1 of each flower variation)

Sew Flower #1 unit from step 1 between one 11½" x 4¾" and one 11½" x 1¾" Fabric B piece as shown. Press.

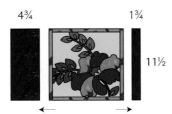

Sew Flower #2 unit from step 1 between one 11½" x 1¾" and one 11½" x 4¾" Fabric B piece as shown. Press.

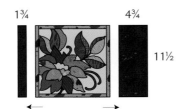

Sew Flower #3 unit from step 1 between one 11½" x 4¼" and one 11½" x 2¼" Fabric B piece as shown. Press.

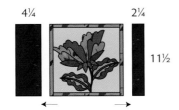

Referring to photo on page 69 and layout, sew Flower #2 unit from step 3 between two 1½" x 17" Fabric B strips. Press seams toward Fabric B.

Referring to photo on page 69 and layout, sew unit from step 5 between Flower #1 unit from step 2 and Flower #3 unit from step 4. Press seams toward center.

Sew two 1¾" x 17" Fabric B strips to top and bottom of unit from step 6. Press.

Fold and press one 1" x 17" Fabric D strip in half lengthwise, wrong sides together to make mock piping. Make two. Place one folded strip, right sides together, along top edge of unit from step 7 matching raw edges, position and sew strip to unit. Do not press. Repeat to position and sew remaining folded strip to bottom of unit.

Referring to step 8 and using 1" x 38" Fabric D strips, fold, press, position, and sew mock piping to sides of unit. Do not press.

0. Referring to Adding the Borders on page 94, sew two 2½" x 17" Fabric B strips to top and bottom of quilt. Press seams toward border.

1. Sew three 2½" x 42" Fabric B strips together end-to-end to make one continuous 2½"-wide Fabric B strip. Measure quilt through center from top to bottom including border just added. Cut two 2½"-wide Fabric B strips to this measurement. Sew to sides of quilt. Press.

Flamboyant Flower
Wall Quilt
Finished Size: 21½" x 42½"

All the emphasis is on the colorful and fanciful flowers on this striking and sophisticated wall quilt. Beads add even more bling to this eye-catching accessory.

Layering and Finishing

1. Trim backing to 25" x 46". Referring to Layering the Quilt on page 94, arrange and baste backing, batting, and top together. Hand or machine quilt as desired.

2. Referring to Binding the Quilt on page 94, sew 2¾" x 42" binding strips end-to-end to make one continuous 2¾"-wide binding strip. Bind quilt to finish. Add beads and other embellishments as desired.

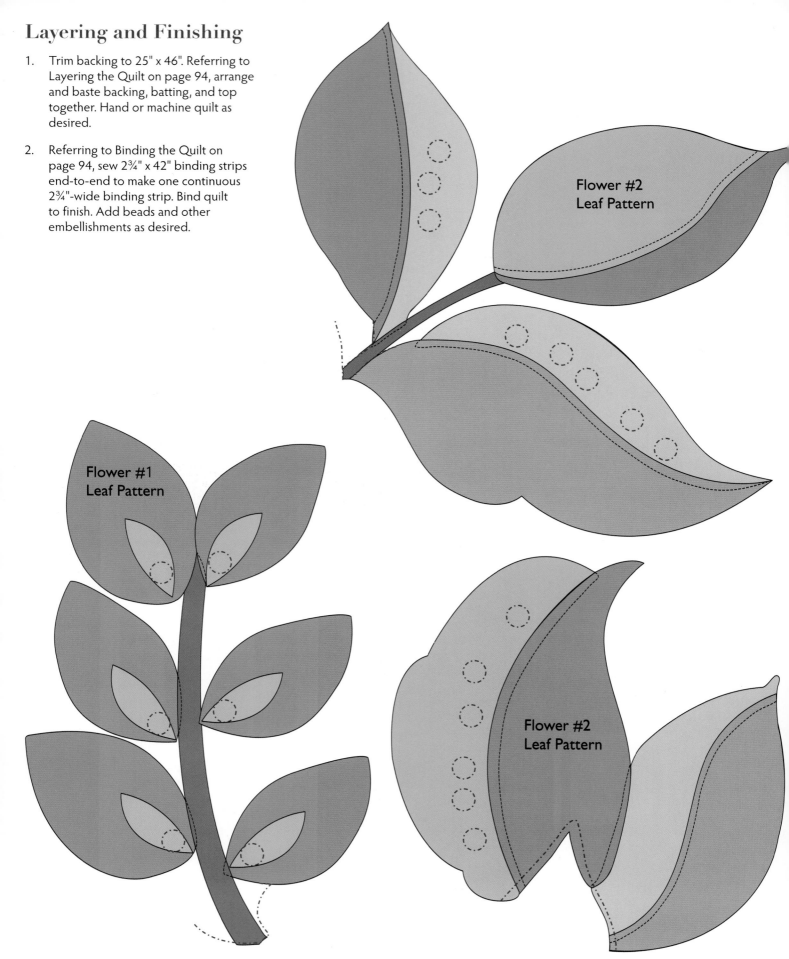

Flower #2
Leaf Pattern

Flower #1
Leaf Pattern

Flower #2
Leaf Pattern

Flower #1
Pattern

Flower #1
Leaf Pattern

Flamboyant Flowers
Patterns are reversed for use
with Quick-Fuse Applique (page 93)

Tracing Line ——————
Tracing Line ----------------------------
(will be hidden behind other fabrics)
Placement Line — ·· — ·· — ·· —

Permission is granted by Debbie Mumm Inc.
to copy pages 72-75 to successsfully
complete project.

Flower #2
Pattern

Flamboyant Flowers
Patterns are reversed for use
with Quick-Fuse Applique (page 93)

Tracing Line ——————
Tracing Line ----------------------
(will be hidden behind other fabrics)
Placement Line —·—·—·—·—·—

Flower #3
Leaf Pattern
Make 2

Flower #3
Pattern

FULL BLOOM
Pillow

These impressive floral pillows make a bold statement in your décor, yet they are simple to construct.

Making the Pillow

Refer to appliqué instructions on page 93. Our instructions are for Quick-Fuse Appliqué, but if you prefer hand appliqué, reverse templates and add ¼"-wide seam allowance.

1. Use Flamboyant Flowers Pattern #2 (page 74) and enlarge by 200% for this project. Trace flower on paper side of fusible web. Use appropriate fabrics to prepare all appliqués for fusing. **Note:** Flamboyant Flower #1 or #3 can be enlarged and substituted if desired.

2. Refer to photo and layout to position and fuse appliqués to 16½" square background fabric piece. Trim excess appliqué fabric even with square. Finish appliqué edges with machine satin stitch or other decorative stitching as desired.

3. Refer to Finishing Pillows on page 95, step 1, to prepare pillow top for quilting. Quilt as desired. Add buttons and other embellishments as desired to quilted pillow top.

4. Use two 11" x 16½" backing pieces and refer to Finishing Pillows page 95, steps 2-4, to sew backing.

5. Insert 16" pillow form or refer to Pillow Forms, page 95, to make pillow form if desired.

SUPPLIES

- **Background and Backing fabric**— ⅝ yard
  One 16½" square
  Two 11" x 16½" pieces
- **Appliqués Flower & Stems**—Assorted scraps
- **Lightweight Fusible Web**—½ yard
- **Buttons**—Assorted
- **Pillow Form 16"**
  OR Optional Pillow Form - ½ yard
  Two 16½" Fabric Squares
  Polyester Fiberfill

FANCIFUL
Pillow

Making the Pillow

Refer to Quick Corner Triangles on page 92. Making a quick corner triangle unit, sew one 12½" Fabric A square to one 14½" Fabric B square as shown. Press.

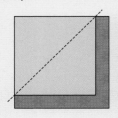

Fabric A = 12½ x 12½
Fabric B = 14½ x 14½

Refer to Quick-Fuse Appliqué on page 93, draw ½" x 20" rectangle on paper-side of fusible web. Cut approximately ¼" outside traced line, fuse to wrong side of 1½" x 22" Fabric C piece, cut on traced line. Referring to layout, fuse strip along Fabric A triangle seam line. Edgestitch in place.

Adding the Appliqués

Refer to appliqué instructions on page 93. Our instructions are for Quick-Fuse Appliqué, but if you prefer hand appliqué, add ¼"-wide seam allowance.

Use Fanciful Pillow patterns to trace leaves and circles on paper side of fusible web. Use appropriate fabrics to prepare all appliqués for fusing.

Refer to photo on page 76 and layout to position and fuse appliqués to pillow top. Finish appliqué edges with machine satin stitch or other decorative stitching as desired. **Note:** We fused and stitched one yellow circle on top of one red circle for added interest.

Finishing the Pillow

Refer to Finishing Pillows on page 95, step 1, to prepare pillow top for quilting. Quilt as desired. Add buttons and other embellishments as desired.

Use two 10" x 14½" Fabric B backing pieces and refer to Finishing Pillows, page 95, steps 2-4 to sew backing.

Insert 14" pillow form or refer to Pillow Forms, page 95, to make a pillow form if desired.

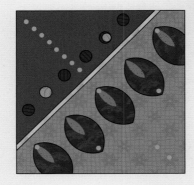

- Fabric A Dark Triangle—½ yard
  One 12½" square
- Fabric B Background and Backing—½ yard
  One 14½" square
  Two 10" x 14½" pieces
- Fabric C Yellow Accent Strip—⅛ yard
  One 1½" x 22"
- Appliqué Leaves and Circles—Assorted scraps
- Lightweight Fusible Web—¼ yard
- Pillow Form 14"
  OR Optional Pillow Form - ½ yard
  Two 14½" Fabric Squares
  Polyester Fiberfill

Fanciful Pillow
Quick-Fuse Applique (page 93)

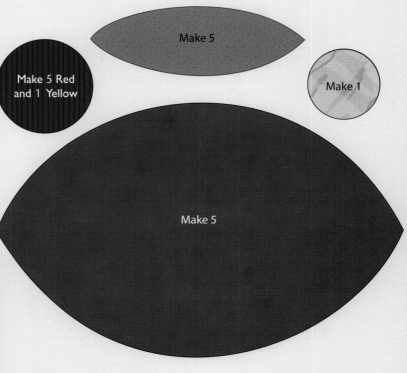

Make 5

Make 1

Make 5 Red and 1 Yellow

Make 5

FLAMBOYANT
Lamp

A flamboyant boudoir requires a bedside lamp with color and personality and this lamp has both in abundance. Pair it with our pretty Bling Box for a tabletop treat for the eyes.

Making the Shade

Tie yarn end onto metal hardware inside lamp, then wrap yarn around lamp shade as shown until shade is covered with yarn. The yarn adds interesting texture to the shade and you can leave it as is, or further embellish it as we did.

To further embellish, count off about ten strands of yarn and wrap strands with a wire. Thread a bead onto wire and twist ends to secure. Clip off extra wire. We chose to alternate between high and low placement of wire/beads and we used an assortment of bead shapes but all in the same color.

Continue wiring groups of yarn strands and adding beads until lamp shade is complete.

Making the Lamp Base

Paint lamp base color desired. Two or more coats may be needed for good coverage. Allow to dry thoroughly between coats of paint. Mix burnt umber acrylic paint with clear glaze in a 1 part paint to 3 parts glaze ratio. You will only need a small amount for this project. Apply glaze to lamp base, adding more glaze where a darker tone is desired and using a damp soft cloth to remove glaze where needed. Allow to dry thoroughly.

Spray lamp base with gloss varnish to finish.

- **Lamp Base***
- **Lamp Shade***
- **Decorative Yarn****
  (Amount depends on size of shade.
  We used one 2.47 oz skein for this small shade.)
- **Beads**
- **Craft Wire**
- **Acrylic Paint in Choice of Colors**
- **Clear Acrylic Glaze**
- **Burnt Umber or Choice of
  Color Acrylic Paint**
- **Gloss Spray Varnish**

*Many discount and home improvement stores offer a wide variety of lamp bases and shades that can be purchased separately.
**Debbie Mumm Yarn is available at Jo-Ann Fabric and Craft Stores

SUPPLIES

FLAMBOYANT
Bling Box

Carry flamboyant colors and floral concepts to your dressing table with our pretty and fun jewelry box. Dimensional paint creates the eye-catching flourishes.

Making the Box

1. Remove any hardware from box and lightly sand. Remove sanding residue with damp cloth. Refer to General Painting Directions on page 95. Allow paint to dry thoroughly between each paint application. Base coat box with Eggplant paint. Several coats may be needed for good coverage. Allow to dry thoroughly.

2. Dampen sea sponge with water and wring thoroughly. Dip sponge in Lavender paint then Eggplant paint. Blot on a paper towel. Using a tapping motion, sponge color onto box, applying lightly for a mottled effect. Sponge a little more Egg Plant toward edges of sides to deepen color.

3. Dry brush Purple and a small amount of Lavender on lid of box. To dry brush, load brush with small amount of paint then blot several times on paper towel until only a small amount of paint remains. Use short strokes in multiple directions to add texture to lid.

4. Determine stencil placement. Use Scotch Magic Tape to hold stencil in place. Using palette knife, spread dimensional paint onto stencil being careful to cover all areas desired and to not move stencil. While dimensional paint is still wet, remove stencil carefully, pulling it straight off to avoid smearing. Clean and dry stencil before moving it to the next area. Continue applying stenciled designs as desired. Allow to dry thoroughly.

5. If desired, deepen color on stenciled areas by painting with Hauser Green Light.

6. Paint any decorative trim Antique White and allow to dry. Following manufacturer's directions, apply Antiquing Medium to Antique White trim and stenciled areas to add shadowing and texture.

7. When box is completely dry, spray with one or two coats of gloss varnish. Allow to dry thoroughly. Glue on beads as desired.

SUPPLIES

- **Unfinished Wooden Box**
- **Delta Ceramcoat® Acrylic Craft Paints**
  Lavender, Eggplant, Purple
- **Americana® Acrylic Craft Paints**
  Antique White, Hauser Green Light
- **Delta Texture Magic™ Dimensional Paint™**
  Spring Green
- **FolkArt® Antiquing Medium by Plaid®**
  Woodn' Bucket Brown
- **Palette Knife**
- **Stencil**
- **Assorted Paintbrushes**
- **Sea Sponge**
- **Assorted Beads and Bead Glue**
- **Sandpaper and Cloth**
- **Gloss Spray Varnish**
- **Scotch® Magic™ Tape**

A compelling combination of spicy Southwest desert colors, this warm-hued palette moves from coffee to clay with bursts of succulent greens and sky blue. Far from being desolate, the desert is a kaleidoscope of color and texture.

DESERT
Dimensions

DESERT Landscape

Desert Landscape Bed Quilt Finished Size: 73"x 97"	FIRST CUT		SECOND CUT	
	Number of Strips or Pieces	Dimensions	Number of Pieces	Dimensions
BLUE				
B-1 ½ yard	2	7" x 42"	6	7" squares
B-2 ½ yard	2	7" x 42"	6	7" squares
B-3 ¼ yard	1	7" x 42"	3	7" squares
B-4 ¼ yard	1	7" x 42"	3	7" squares
B-5 ½ yard	2	7" x 42"	6	7" squares
B-6 ½ yard	2	7" x 42"	6	7" squares
BROWN				
BR-1 ½ yard	2	7" x 42"	8	7" squares
BR-2 ½ yard	2	7" x 42"	8	7" squares
BR-3 ⅔ yard	3	7" x 42"	12	7" squares
BR-4 ⅔ yard	3	7" x 42"	15	7" squares
BR-5 ⅞ yard	4	7" x 42"	18	7" squares
BR-6 ⅞ yard	4	7" x 42"	18	7" squares
BR-7 ¼ yard	1	7" x 42"	3	7" squares
GREEN				
G-1 ½ yard	2	7" x 42"	10	7" squares
G-2 ½ yard	2	7" x 42"	10	7" squares
G-3 ½ yard	2	7" x 42"	10	7" squares
G-4 ½ yard	2	7" x 42"	10	7" squares
G-5 ½ yard	2	7" x 42"	8	7" squares
ORANGE				
O-1 ½ yard	2	7" x 42"	7	7" squares
O-2 ⅔ yard	3	7" x 42"	15	7" squares
O-3 ½ yard	2	7" x 42"	8	7" squares
O-4 ½ yard	2	7" x 42"	6	7" squares
O-5 ½ yard	2	7" x 42"	7	7" squares
O-6 ½ yard	2	7" x 42"	7	7" squares
O-7 ½ yard	2	7" x 42"	8	7" squares
O-8 ½ yard	2	7" x 42"	6	7" squares
Binding ¾ yard		2¾"- wide bias strips to equal 360" OR		
	9	2¾" x 42"		

Backing - 6¾ yards
Batting - 81" x 105"

Fabric Requirements and Cutting Instructions

Read all instructions before beginning and use ¼"-wide seam allowance throughout. Read Cutting Strips and Pieces on page 92 prior to cutting fabric.

Getting Started

The striking hues of the desert landscape radiate throughout this bed quilt. Each multi-colored block measures 12½" square (unfinished). Refer to Accurate Seam Allowance on page 92. Whenever possible use the Assembly Line Method on page 92. Press seam in the direction of arrows.

Making the Single Block Rows

Rows 1, 2, 3, and 6 use a single repeating block in each row construction. When sewing blocks together to make rows, press even rows to the right and odd rows to the left. Blocks measure 12½" square (unfinished).

1. Draw a diagonal line on wrong side of one 7" Fabric B-2 square. Place marked square and one 7" Fabric B-6 square right sides together. Sew scant ¼" away from drawn line on **both** sides to make half-square triangles as shown. Make three. Cut **on** drawn line and press. This will make six half-square triangle units. Repeat to make six half-square triangles in each of the following combinations: B-3/B-1, B-6/B-5, and B-4/B-5. Square units to 6½".

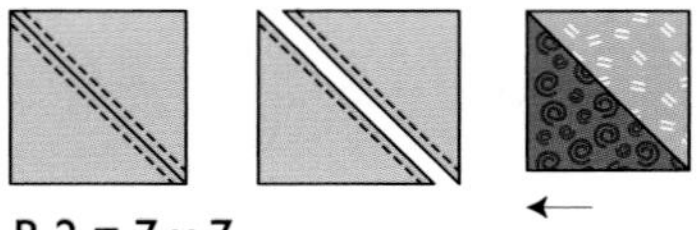

B-2 = 7 x 7
B-6 = 7 x 7
Make 3

Square to 6½
Make 6
Half-square triangles

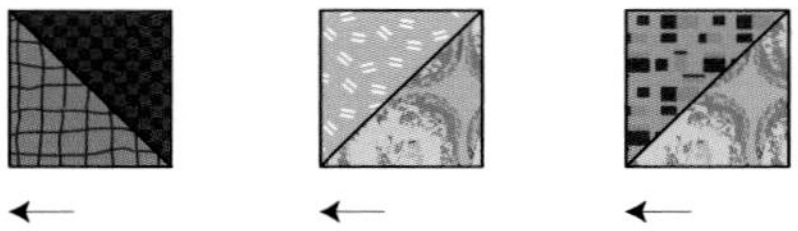

B-3/B-1
Make 6

B-6/B-5
Make 6

B-4/B-5
Make 6

Sew four units from step 1, one of each combination, together as shown. Refer to Twisting Seams on page 92. Press. Make six. Block measures 12½" square.

Row 1 Block

Make 6
Block measures
12½" square

Referring to photo on page 81 and layout, arrange and sew blocks from step 2 together to make Row 1. Press.

Refer to step 1 to make six half-square triangles in each of the following combinations: G-2/B-1, BR-6/G-1, B-2/G-4, and G-3/BR-7. Sew four units, one of each combination, together as shown. Twist Seam. Press. Make six. Referring to photo on page 81 and layout, arrange and sew blocks together to make Row 2. Press.

G-2/B-1	BR-6/G-1	B-2/G-4	G-3/BR-7
Make 6	Make 6	Make 6	Make 6

Row 2 Block

Make 6
Block measures 12½" square

Refer to step 1 to make six half-square triangles in each of the following combinations: O-6/O-8, BR-5/O-5, O-8/O-2, and O-1/BR-6. Sew four units, one of each combination, together as shown. Twist Seam. Press. Make six. Referring to photo on page 81 and layout, arrange and sew blocks together to make Row 3. Press.

O-6/O-8	BR-5/O-5	O-8/O-2	O-1/BR-6
Make 6	Make 6	Make 6	Make 6

Row 3 Block

Make 6
Block measures 12½" square

Desert Landscape
Bed Quilt

Finished Size: 73" x 97"

Rich colors and a creative arrangement paint a striking desert scene using just one technique—easy half-square triangles. This bed-size quilt will make a bold and beautiful statement in any setting.

6. Refer to step 1 to make six half-square triangles in each of the following combinations: G-2/O-4, BR-5/G-1, O-4/G-3, and G-4/BR-4. Sew four units, one of each combination, together as shown. Twist Seam. Press. Make six. Block measures 12½" square. Referring to photo on page 81 and layout, arrange and sew blocks together to make Row 6. Press.

G-2/O-4
Make 6

BR-5/G-1
Make 6

O-4/G-3
Make 6

G-4/BR-4
Make 6

Row 6 Block

Make 6
Block measures 12½" square

Making the Alternating Block Rows

To add interest to our quilt, each of the following rows uses two alternating blocks for construction. When sewing blocks together to make rows, press seams in even rows to the right and odd rows to the left. All blocks in each row measures 12½" square (unfinished).

1. Draw a diagonal line on wrong side of one 7" Fabric O-1 square. Place marked square and one 7" Fabric O-7 square right sides together. Sew scant ¼" away from drawn line on **both** sides to make half-square triangles as shown. Make two. Cut **on** drawn line and press. This will make four half-square triangle units; three will be used for this project. Repeat to make three half-square triangles in each of the following combinations: BR-3/O-2, O-7/O-6, and O-5/BR-4. Square units to 6½".

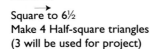

O-1 = 7 x 7
O-7 = 7 x 7
Make 2

Square to 6½
Make 4 Half-square triangles
(3 will be used for project)

BR-3/O-2
Make 3

O-7/O-6
Make 3

O-5/BR-4
Make 3

2. Sew four units from step 1, one of each combination, together as shown. Refer to Twisting Seams page 92. Press. Make three.

Row 4-A Block

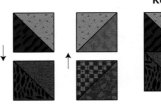

Make 3
Block measures 12½" square

3. Refer to step 1 to make three half-square triangle units each with the following combinations: O-2/O-7, BR-3/O-1, O-7/O-6, and O-5/BR-4. Sew four units, one of each combination, together as shown. Twist Seam. Press. Make three. Referring to photo on page 81 and layout on page 83, arrange and sew Blocks 4-A and 4-B together, alternating blocks to make Row 4. Press.

O-2/O-7
Make 3

BR-3/O-1
Make 3

O-7/O-6
Make 3

O-5/BR-4
Make 3

Row 4-B Block

Make 3
Block measures 12½" square

4. Refer to step 1 to make three half-square triangle units each with the following combinations: G-4/G-5, BR-6/G-3, G-5/G-1 and G-2/BR-5. Sew four units, one of each combination, together as shown. Twist Seam. Press. Make three.

G-4/G-5
Make 3

BR-6/G-3
Make 3

G-5/G-1
Make 3

G-2/BR-5
Make 3

Row 5-A Block

Make 3
Block measures 12½" square

Refer to step 1 to make three half-square triangle units each with the following combinations: G-4/G-5, BR-6/G-3, G-5/G-2, and G-1/BR-5. Sew four units, one of each combination, together as shown. Twist Seam. Press. Make three. Referring to photo on page 81 and layout on page 83, arrange and sew Blocks 5-A and 5-B together together alternating blocks to make Row 5. Press.

G-4/G-5
Make 3
BR-6/G-3
Make 3
G-5/G-2
Make 3
G-1/BR-5
Make 3

Row 5-B Block

Make 3
Block measures 12½" square

Refer to step 1 to make three half-square triangle units each with the following combinations: BR-4/O-3, BR-2/BR-3, O-3/BR-6, and BR-5/BR-2. Sew four units, one of each combination, together as shown. Twist Seam. Press. Make three.

BR-4/O-3
Make 3
BR-2/BR-3
Make 3
O-3/BR-6
Make 3
BR-5/BR-2
Make 3

Row 7-A Block

Make 3
Block measures 12½" square

7. Refer to step 1 to make three half-square triangle units each with the following combinationss: BR-3/O-3, BR-2/BR-4, O-3/BR-5, and BR-6/BR-2. Sew four units, one of each combination, together as shown. Twist Seam. Press. Make three. Referring to photo on page 81 and layout on page 83, arrange and sew Blocks 7-A and 7-B together, alternating blocks to make Row 7. Press.

BR-3/O-3
Make 3
BR-2/BR-4
Make 3
O-3/BR-5
Make 3
BR-6/BR-2
Make 3

Row 7-B Block

Make 3
Block measures 12½" square

8. Refer to step 1 to make three half-square triangle units each with the following combinations: BR-4/O-2, BR-1/BR-3, O-2/BR-6, and BR-5/BR-1. Sew four units, one of each combination, together as shown. Twist Seam. Press. Make three.

BR-4/O-2
Make 3
BR-1/BR-3
Make 3
O-2/BR-6
Make 3
BR-5/BR-1
Make 3

Row 8-A Block

Make 3
Block measures 12½" square

9. Refer to step 1 to make three half-square triangle units each with the following combinations: BR-3/O-2, BR-1/BR-4, O-2/BR-5, and BR-6/BR-1. Sew four units, one of each combination, together as shown. Twist Seam. Press. Make three. Referring to photo on page 81 and layout on page 83, arrange and sew Blocks 8-A and 8-B together, alternating blocks to make Row 8. Press.

BR-3/O-2
Make 3
BR-1/BR-4
Make 3
O-2/BR-5
Make 3
BR-6/BR-1
Make 3

Row 8-B Block

Make 3
Block measures 12½" square

Finishing the Quilt

1. Referring to photo on page 81 and layout on page 83, arrange and sew together Rows 1-8. Press.

2. Cut backing crosswise into three equal pieces. Sew pieces together lengthwise to make one 81" x 120" (approximate) backing piece. Press and trim to 81" x 105".

3. Referring to Layering the Quilt on page 94, arrange and baste backing, batting, and top together. Hand or machine quilt as desired.

4. Refer to Making Bias Strips page 94, to cut 2¾"-wide strips. Sew 2¾" x 42" binding strips end-to-end to make one continuous 2¾"-wide binding strip. Refer to Binding the Quilt on page 94 and bind quilt to finish.

DESERT Flower

Desert Flower Wall Quilt Finished Size: 41"x 41"	FIRST CUT		SECOND CUT	
	Number of Strips or Pieces	Dimensions	Number of Pieces	Dimensions
Fabric A Dark Squares ⅔ yard	2	10½" x 42"	5	10½" squares
Fabric B Dark Squares ⅔ yard	2	10½" x 42"	4	10½" squares
Fabric C Block Sashing ⅓ yard	8	1" x 42"	2 / 4 / 6	1" x 32½" / 1" x 31½" / 1" x 10½"
Fabric D Prairie Points ¾ yard	5	4½" x 42"	36	4½" squares
First Border ⅙ yard	4	1" x 42"	2 / 2	1" x 33½" / 1" x 32½"
Outside Border ½ yard	4	4" x 42"	2 / 2	4" x 40½" / 4" x 33½"
Binding ½ yard	5	2¾" x 42"		

Backing - 2⅝ yards

Batting - 47" x 47"

Large Flower Appliqués - ¼ yard each of three fabrics

Stem, Leaves & Small Flower Appliqués - Assorted scraps

Lightweight Fusible Web - 1 yard

Assorted Beads

Fabric Requirements and Cutting Instructions

Read all instructions before beginning and use ¼"-wide seam allowance throughout. Read Cutting Strips and Pieces on page 92 prior to cutting fabric.

Getting Started

Desert plants bloom in the arid landscape briefly bringing vivid color to the desert's subtle beauty. This quilt is simple to make using quick fused appliqué technique for the flowers, easy block assembly, and folded dimensional Prairie Points. Refer to Accurate Seam Allowance on page 92. Whenever possible use the Assembly Line Method on page 92. Press seams in direction of arrows.

Adding the Appliqués

Refer to appliqué instructions on page 93. Our instructions are for Quick-Fuse Appliqué, but if you prefer hand appliqué, reverse templates and add ¼"-wide seam allowance.

1. Use patterns on pages 88-89 to trace flowers, stems, and leaves on paper side of fusible web. Use appropriate fabrics to prepare all appliqués for fusing.

2. Refer to photo to position and fuse Cactus Bloom Appliqués to five 10½" Fabric A squares. Position and fuse Desert Vine Appliqués to four 10½" Fabric B squares. Finish appliqué edges with machine satin stitch or other decorative stitching as desired.

Assembly

1. Arrange and sew together two Cactus Bloom blocks, two 1" x 10½" Fabric C pieces, and one Desert Vine block as shown. Press. Make two.

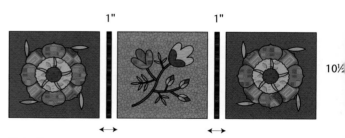

1"   1"   10½"

Make 2

2. Arrange and sew together two Desert Vine blocks, two 1" x 10½" Fabric C pieces, and one Cactus Bloom block as shown. Press.

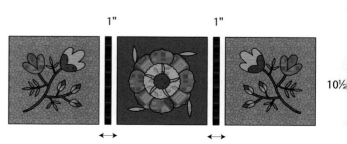

1"   1"   10½"

3. Referring to photo, arrange and sew together four 1" x 31½" Fabric C strips and rows from steps 1 and 2. Press seams toward Fabric C.

4. Referring to photo, sew two 1" x 32½" Fabric C strips to sides of quilt. Press seams toward Fabric C.

Adding the Borders

1. Sew quilt between two 1" x 32½" First Border strips. Press seams toward border. Sew two 1" x 33½" First Border strips to sides of quilt. Press.

2. Fold and press one 4½" Fabric D square in half diagonally, wrong sides together. Fold and press diagonally in half again, as shown, to make Prairie Point. Raw edges will be together. Make thirty-six.

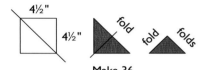

3. Arrange and baste nine Prairie Points along top edge of quilt, overlapping and matching raw edges. Repeat to arrange and baste nine Prairie Points each to bottom and sides of quilt. Keep Prairie Points in this position, points towards center, while sewing Outside Border strips.

4. Sew two 4" x 33½" Outside Border strips to top and bottom of quilt. Press Outside Border and Prairie Point seams toward First Border. Sew two 4" x 40½" Outside Borders strips to sides of quilt. Press seam allowances toward First Border.

Layering and Finishing

1. Cut backing crosswise into two equal pieces. Sew pieces together lengthwise to make one 47" x 80" (approximate) backing piece. Press and trim to 47" x 47".

2. Referring to Layering the Quilt on page 94, arrange and baste backing, batting, and top together. Hand or machine quilt as desired.

3. Refer to Binding the Quilt on page 94. Sew 2¾" x 42" binding strips end-to-end to make one continuous 2¾"-wide binding strip. Bind quilt to finish.

4. Referring to photo and appliqué patterns on pages 88-89, embellish quilt with beads as desired.

Desert Flower
Wall Quilt
Finished Size: 41" x 41"

Desert flowers bloom on subtle, sandy backgrounds on this charming wall quilt that will add a decorator's touch to your home. Bead embellishment and prairie points complete this beautiful wall quilt.

Desert Vine Appliqué
Make 2
and 2 Reversed

Catcus Bloom Appliqué
Make 5

Desert Flower Wall Quilt
Patterns are reversed for use
with Quick-Fuse Appliqué (page 93)

Tracing Line _____
Tracing Line ----------------------
(will be hidden behind other fabrics)
Placement Line _._._._._._._

DESERT
Mosaic Planter

The earthy beauty and textures of the desert are expressed in this handsome and useful mosaic flowerpot.

Making the Planter

Refer to photo as needed. Refer to Mosaic Safety Precautions on page 95 before beginning this project.

1. Place one or two same color tiles in a zip-lock plastic bag. Place plastic bag on hard surface. Wearing safety glasses and being careful not to split plastic bag, hit tiles with hammer, breaking them into random-sized small pieces. Continue breaking tiles as needed for design; sorting them by color on work surface.

2. Following manufacturer's directions, spread mastic on one side of flowerpot. Leaving ⅛" to ¼" between pieces, fit tiles together in a mosaic pattern, changing from one color to another as desired.

3. We chose to create a design using pre-cut decorative border triangles on a portion of our planter as shown in the photo at right. Large glass gems enhanced the design.

4. We also used decorative colored rocks in several different ways: as a diagonal divider between tile treatments and to create triangular designs among the tile pieces.

5. Continue adding mastic and adhere tile pieces, rocks, and gems as desired.

6. Clean off any excess mastic and allow to dry 48 hours.

7. Using a putty knife, spread grout into all spaces between tiles, rocks, gems and around edges.

8. Wearing rubber gloves, use sponge to wipe off excess grout. Wipe flat across the surface and rinse and wring sponge in a bucket thoroughly after each pass. Make sure that outer surface of all tile, rock, and gem pieces are clear of grout and that all spaces in between are covered with grout. **Note:** Do not put grout down the drain. Use a bucket of water when cleaning tile and tools.

9. When excess grout is removed, use a soft cloth (rinsing often) to carefully clear the top of each tile, gem, and rock.

10. Mist the surface with water several times as the grout cures to avoid cracking. Allow to cure for 3 days.

11. If grout didn't include a sealer, apply grout sealer according to manufacturer's directions.

DESERT
Mosaic Stepping Stone

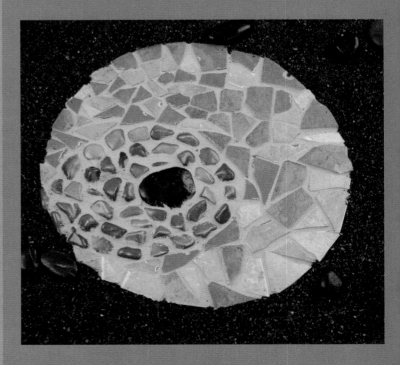

Making the Stepping Stone

Step out in style by making stepping stones using the same techniques as the mosaic planter. Read Mosaic Safety Precautions on page 95 before beginning this project.

Purchase a concrete stepping stone at a discount or home improvement store. These stepping stones come in different shapes and sizes and any will work as long as the top surface is flat.

For an outdoor project, use Thinset (a concrete product) instead of mastic. Following package directions, mix thinset in a small container with an airtight lid. Use a palette knife or putty knife to spread thinset onto tile pieces, rocks, and gems while placing them. Clean out any thinset that is sticking up between the pieces. Allow to dry 24 hours.

Refer to Dessert Mosaic Planter steps 7-11 to grout stepping stone. Place stepping stone in the garden after making sure that there are no sharp edges to cut bare feet. If sharp edges are a problem, use an emery board to file them smooth.

SUPPLIES

Terracotta Flowerpot
Tile Mastic
Putty Knife or Mastic Spreader
Pre-Mixed Grout* - Sanded Grey
Grout Sponge
Decorative Rocks**
4" Square Tiles in Earth Colors
(We used ten for an 8" pot)
Decorative Border Tile Strip (Optional)
Large Glass Gems (Optional)
Hammer, Zip-Lock Plastic Bags, Safety Glasses

*Look for a pre-mixed grout that includes a sealer; or purchase grout sealer separately.
**Available at craft stores.

GENERAL Directions

Cutting Strips and Pieces

We recommend washing cotton fabrics in cold water and pressing before making projects in this book. Using a rotary cutter, see-through ruler, and a cutting mat, cut the strips and pieces for the project. If indicated on the Cutting Chart, some will need to be cut again into smaller strips and pieces. Make second cuts in order shown to maximize use of fabric. The yardage amounts and cutting instructions are based on an approximate fabric width of 42".

Pressing

Pressing is very important for accurate seam allowances. Press seams using either steam or dry heat with an "up and down" motion. Do not use side-to-side motion as this will distort the unit or block. Set the seam by pressing along the line of stitching, then press seams to one side as indicated by project instructions and diagram arrows.

Twisting Seams

When a block has several seams meeting in the center as shown, there will be less bulk if seam allowances are pressed in a circular type direction and the center intersection "twisted". Remove 1-2 stitches in the seam allowance to enable the center to twist and lay flat. This technique aids in quilt assembly by allowing the seams to fall opposite each other when repeated blocks are next to each other. The technique works well with 4-patch blocks, pinwheel blocks, and quarter-square triangle blocks.

Accurate Seam Allowance

Accurate seam allowances are always important, but especially when the blocks contain many pieces and the quilt top contains multiple pieced borders. If each seam is off as little as 1/16", you'll soon find yourself struggling with components that just won't fit.

To ensure seams are a perfect 1/4"-wide, try this simple test: Cut three strips of fabric, each exactly 1½" x 12". With right sides together, and long raw edges aligned, sew two strips together, carefully maintaining a 1/4" seam. Press seam to one side. Add the third strip to complete the strip set. Press and measure. The finished strip set should measure 3½" x 12". The center strip should measure 1"-wide, the two outside strips 1¼"-wide, and the seam allowances exactly 1/4".

If your measurements differ, check to make sure that seams have been pressed flat. If strip set still doesn't "measure up," try stitching a new strip set, adjusting the seam allowance until a perfect 1/4"-wide seam is achieve.

Assembly Line Method

Whenever possible, use an assembly line method. Position pieces right sides together and line up next to sewing machine. Stitch first unit together, then continue sewing others without breaking threads. When all units are sewn, clip threads to separate. Press seams in the direction of arrows.

Quick Corner Triangles

Quick corner triangles are formed by simpl sewing fabric squares to other squares or rectangles. The directions and diagrams with each project illustrate what size pieces to use and where to place squares on the corresponding piece. Follow steps 1–3 below to make quick corner triangle units.

1. With pencil and ruler, draw diagonal line on wrong side of fabric square that will form the triangle. This will be your sewing line.

   Sewing line

2. With right sides together, place square on corresponding piece. Matching raw edges, pin in place, and sew ON drawn line. Trim off exces fabric, leaving 1/4"-wide seam allowance as shown.

   Trim 1/4" away from sewing line

3. Press seam in direction of arrow as shown in step-by-step project diagram. Measure completed quick corner triangle unit to ensure the greatest accuracy.

   Finished quick corner triangle unit

Fussy Cut

To make a "fussy cut," carefully position rule or template over a selected design in fabric Include seam allowances before cutting desired pieces.

Quick-Fuse Appliqué

Quick-fuse appliqué is a method of adhering appliqué pieces to a background with fusible web. For quick and easy results, simply quick-fuse appliqué pieces in place. Use sewable, lightweight fusible web for the projects in this book unless otherwise indicated. Finish raw edges with stitching as desired. Laundering is not recommended unless edges are finished.

With paper side up, lay fusible web over appliqué pattern. Leaving ½" space between pieces, trace all elements of design. Cut around traced pieces, approximately ¼" outside traced line.

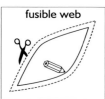
fusible web

With paper side up, position and press fusible web to wrong side of selected fabrics. Follow manufacturer's directions for iron temperature and fusing time. Cut out each piece on traced line.

fabric-wrong side

Remove paper backing from pieces. A thin film will remain on wrong side of fabric. Position and fuse all pieces of one appliqué design at a time onto background, referring to photos for placement. Fused design will be the reverse of traced pattern.

Appliqué Pressing Sheet

An appliqué pressing sheet is very helpful when there are many small elements to apply using a quick-fuse appliqué technique. The pressing sheet allows small items to be bonded together before applying them to the background. The sheet is coated with a special material that prevents fusible web from adhering permanently to the sheet. Follow manufacturer's directions. Remember to let fabric cool completely before lifting it from the appliqué sheet. If not cooled, the fusible web could remain on the sheet instead of on the fabric.

Machine Appliqué

This technique should be used when you are planning to launder quick-fuse projects. Several different stitches can be used: small narrow zigzag stitch, satin stitch, blanket stitch, or another decorative machine stitch. Use an open toe appliqué foot if your machine has one. Use a stabilizer to obtain even stitches and help prevent puckering. Always practice first to check machine settings.

1. Fuse all pieces following Quick-Fuse Appliqué directions.

2. Cut a piece of stabilizer large enough to extend beyond the area to be stitched. Pin to the wrong side of fabric.

3. Select thread to match appliqué.

4. Following the order that appliqués were positioned, stitch along the edges of each section. Anchor beginning and ending stitches by tying off or stitching in place two or three times.

5. Complete all stitching, then remove stabilizer.

Hand Appliqué

Hand appliqué is easy when you start out with the right supplies. Cotton and machine embroidery thread are easy to work with. Pick a color that matches the appliqué fabric as closely as possible. Use appliqué or silk pins for holding shapes in place and a long, thin needle, such as a sharp, for stitching.

1. Make a template for every shape in the appliqué design. Use a dotted line to show where pieces overlap.

2. Place template on right side of appliqué fabric. Trace around template.

3. Cut out shapes ¼" beyond traced line.

4. Position shapes on background fabric, referring to quilt layout. Pin shapes in place.

5. When layering and stitching appliqué shapes, always work from background to foreground. Where shapes overlap, do not turn under and stitch edges of bottom pieces. Turn and stitch the edges of the piece on top.

6. Use the traced line as your turn-under guide. Entering from the wrong side of the appliqué shape, bring the needle up on the traced line. Using the tip of the needle, turn under the fabric along the traced line. Using blind stitch, stitch along folded edge to join the appliqué shape to the background fabric. Turn under and stitch about ¼" at a time.

Embroidery Stitch Guide

French Knot

Satin Stitch

Stem Stitch

Primitive Stitch

Running Stitch

Fly Stitch

Big Stitch

Lazy Daisy Stitch

Blanket Stitch

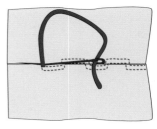
Blind Stitch

Adding the Borders

1. Measure quilt through the center from side to side. Trim two border strips to this measurement. Sew to top and bottom of quilt. Press seams toward border.

2. Measure quilt through the center from top to bottom, including borders added in step 1. Trim border strips to this measurement. Sew to sides and press. Repeat to add additional borders.

Layering the Quilt

1. Cut backing and batting 4" to 8" larger than quilt top.

2. Lay pressed backing on bottom (right side down), batting in middle, and pressed quilt top (right side up) on top. Make sure everything is centered and that backing and batting are flat. Backing and batting will extend beyond quilt top.

3. Begin basting in center and work toward outside edges. Baste vertically and horizontally, forming a 3"–4" grid. Baste or pin completely around edge of quilt top. Quilt as desired. Remove basting.

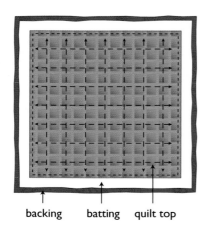

backing   batting   quilt top

Binding the Quilt

1. Trim batting and backing to ¼" beyond raw edge of quilt top. This will add fullness to binding.

2. Join binding strips to make one continuous strip if needed. To join, place strips perpendicular to each other, right sides together, and draw a line. Sew on drawn line and trim triangle extensions, leaving a ¼"-wide seam allowance. Continue stitching ends together to make the desired length. Press seams open.

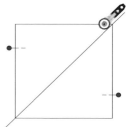

←trim

3. Fold and press binding strips in half lengthwise with wrong sides together.

4. Measure quilt through center from side to side. Cut two binding strips to this measurement. Lay binding strips on top and bottom edges of quilt top with raw edges of binding and quilt top aligned. Sew through all layers, ¼" from quilt edge. Press binding away from quilt top.

Front of Quilt

5. Measure quilt through center from top to bottom, including binding just added. Cut two binding strips to this measurement and sew to sides through all layers, including binding just added. Press.

6. Folding top and bottom first, fold binding around to back then repeat with sides. Press and pin in position. Hand-stitch binding in place using a blind stitch.

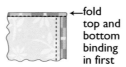

←fold top and bottom binding in first

Making Bias Strips

1. Refer to Fabric Requirements and Cutting Instructions for the amount of fabric required for the specific bias needed.

2. Remove selvages from the fabric piece and cut into a square. Mark edge with straight pin where selvages were removed as shown. Cut square once diagonally into two equal 45° triangles. (For larger squares, fold square in half diagonally and gently press fold. Open fabric square and cut on fold.)

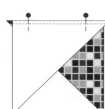

3. Place pinned edges right sides together and stitch along edge with a ¼" seam. Press seam open.

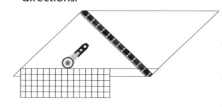

4. Using a ruler and rotary cutter, cut bias strips to width specified in quilt directions.

5. Each strip has a diagonal end. To join, place strips perpendicular to each other right sides together, matching diagonal cut edges and allowing tips of angles to extend approximately ¼" beyond edge. Sew ¼"-wide seams. Continue stitching ends together to make the desired length. Press seams open. Cut strips into recommended lengths according to quilt directions.

Finishing Pillows

Layer batting between pillow top and lining. Baste. Hand or machine quilt as desired, unless otherwise indicated. Trim batting and lining even with raw edge of pillow top.

Narrow hem one long edge of each backing piece by folding under ¼" to wrong side. Press. Fold under ¼" again to wrong side. Press. Stitch along folded edge.

With right sides up, lay one backing piece over second piece so hemmed edges overlap, making backing unit the same measurement as the pillow top. Baste backing pieces together at top and bottom where they overlap.

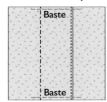

With right sides together, position and pin pillow top to backing. Using ¼"-wide seam, sew around edges, trim corners, turn right side out, and press.

Pillow Forms

Cut two pieces of fabric to finished size of pillow form plus ½". Place right sides together, aligning raw edges. Using ¼"-wide seam, sew around all edges, leaving 4" opening for turning. Trim corners and turn right side out. Stuff to desired fullness with polyester fiberfill and hand-stitch opening closed.

Tips for Felting Wool

Wet wool fabric or WoolFelt™ with hot water. Do not mix colors as dyes may run.

Blot wool with a dry towel and place both towel and wool in dryer on high heat until thoroughly dry. The result is a thicker, fuller fabric that will give added texture to the wool. Pressing felted wool is not recommended, as it will flatten the texture. Most wools will shrink 15-30% when felted, adjust yardage accordingly.

Lacing Stitch

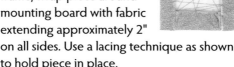

To insert a quilt block or piece of fabric inside a frame, wrap piece around mounting board with fabric extending approximately 2" on all sides. Use a lacing technique as shown to hold piece in place.

Couching Technique

Couching is a method of attaching a textured yarn, cord, or fiber to fabric for decorative purposes. Use an open-toe embroidery foot, couching foot, or a zigzag presser foot and matching or monofilament thread. Sew with a long zigzag stitch just barely wider than the cord or yarn. Stabilizer on the wrong side of fabric is recommended. Place the yarn, cord, or fiber on right side of fabric and zigzag to attach as shown. A hand-stitch can be used if desired.

Couching

General Painting Directions

Read all instructions on paint products before using and carefully follow manufacturer's instructions and warnings. For best results, allow paint to dry thoroughly between each coat and between processes unless directed otherwise. Wear face mask and safety goggles when sanding. Rubber gloves are recommended when handling stains and other finishing products.

Mosaic Safety Precautions

Making mosaics requires basic shop safety practices. Wear goggles when cutting glass. Vacuum carefully after cutting glass to pick up all slivers. Wear rubber dishwashing gloves when applying grout to avoid skin irritation and to protect your hands from sharp corners. Keep materials out of reach of children.

Cutting Glass

1. Cover a flat work surface with several layers of newspaper. Hold cutter however it feels most comfortable. It is essential that the cutter is lubricated each time before scoring glass.

2. Safety glasses and gloves must be worn while working with glass. Stand to score glass which allows clear sight and proper pressure while scoring. Glass is not cut, it is scored, so it doesn't take a lot of strength. By exerting firm but comfortable pressure, the wheel of the cutter scratches the glass, creating a stress point. When pressure is applied to the score line, the glass should break along the line. When cutting colored glass, always score the glass on its smoothest side.

3. On padded surface, hold glass securely with one gloved hand while scoring with the other. Begin to score at the edge of the glass. Maintain an even pressure while scoring. Score line should be visible and a gentle 'ripping' sound should be heard. If no sound is heard or a score line isn't seen, apply more pressure with the next score. A heavy, white, fuzzy line indicates that too much pressure is being used. Different types of glass will require different pressure.

4. Once the glass is scored, hold glass securely with one hand and position the jaws of the pliers parallel to, but not directly on the score line. Make a sharp upward and outward movement and the glass will break along the score line. Practice the technique several times using clear glass scraps before cutting colored glass.

About Debbie Mumm

A talented designer, author, and entrepreneur, Debbie Mumm has been creating charming artwork and quilt designs for more than twenty years.

Debbie got her start in the quilting industry in 1986 with her unique and simple-to-construct quilt patterns. Since that time, she has authored more than fifty books featuring quilting and home decorating projects and has led her business to become a multi-faceted enterprise that includes publishing, fabric design, and licensed art divisions.

Known world-wide for the many licensed products that feature her designs, Debbie loves to bring traditional elements together with fresh palettes and modern themes to create the look of today's country.

Designs by Debbie Mumm

Special thanks to my creative teams:

Editorial & Project Design

Carolyn Ogden: Publications & Marketing Manager
Nancy Kirkland: Seamstress/Quilter • Georgie Gerl: Technical Writer/Editor
Carolyn Lowe: Technical Editor • Jackie Saling: Craft Designer
Anita Pederson: Machine Quilter

Book Design & Production

Tom Harlow: Graphics Manager • Monica Ziegler: Graphic Designer
Kristi Somday: Graphic Designer
Kathy Rickel: Art Studio Assistant • Kris Clifford: Executive Assistant

Photography

Debbie Mumm® Graphics Studio

Art Team

Kathy Arbuckle: Artist/Designer • Gil-Jin Foster: Artist

The Debbie Mumm® Sewing Studio exclusively uses Bernina® sewing machines.
Stock Photography Sources: www.stockxpert.com, www.fotolia.com, www.flickr.com, www.photos.com

©2008 Debbie Mumm

Produced by:
Debbie Mumm, Inc.
1116 E. Westview Court
Spokane, WA 99218
(509) 466-3572
Fax (509) 466-6919

www.debbiemumm.com

Published by:
Leisure Arts, Inc
5701 Ranch Drive
Little Rock, AR • 72223
www.leisurearts.com

Discover More from Debbie Mumm®

Joy Joy Joy
by Debbie Mumm®
96-page, soft cover

Debbie Mumm's®
Greenwood Gardens
96-page, soft cover

Debbie Mumm's®
New Expressions
96-page, soft cover

Memories & Milestones
by Debbie Mumm®
96-page, soft cover

Available at local fabric and craft shops or at **debbiemumm.com**